BROWN COWS
IN THE
MANOR

Richard Hansford

outskirtspress

DENVER, COLORADO

To my loving wife and fellow farmer Rosie. Also to the Miller family for their kind instruction in the art of animal husbandry

DISCLAIMER

This book is a work of non-fiction. Though some names have been changed and the sequence of some events altered, the intent is to give a truthful portrayal of our attempts at farming and horseback riding and to give offense to no-one.

Table of Contents

1

Mud on the Shoes

It is said that Nature abhors a vacuum. No less does my wife Rosie abhor tranquility. It seems to her to be a vacuum in the affairs of Man: a quiet life speaks to her of lost opportunity and even hints at a lack of character. Yet tranquility surrounded us, from the ersatz perfection of the neo-colonial house to the little patches of lawn and the prim and proper march of evergreens along the driveway. We had moved from the vibrant anarchy of the Caribbean island of Grenada to a country retreat in Maryland. The house was in an area which could not make up its mind as to whether it was rural or suburban and the people who lived in the vicinity were mainly recluses. There was a purpose behind their rows of giant Leyland cypress and that was quite evidently to see as little as possible of their fellow man. Behind their evergreen bulwarks they kept at bay the perils of city life, whether real or imagined.

Rosie herself maintained an intense job in public health but she was concerned about me. When her gentle quizzing revealed that my days revolved around putting out the trash and trimming grass with a pair of shears, she reached her limit. I needed more activity in my life, she was sure. In vain I protested that I was working on another, possibly ill-conceived, book.

"We need a farm," she pronounced. "Some cows, possibly a horse or two. We used to have so much fun doing that."

Clouds of *déjà vu* washed over me. As one of my academic friends later reminded me, perhaps it was time to go back and re-read my own book (*The Professor and the Brown Cows*). Didn't Einstein once say that you had to be an idiot to repeat the same experiment and expect a different result?

Yet maybe Rosie was right. Maybe they really had been good times. It was true that a decade had passed and we were weaker in our muscles and creakier in our joints. Hay bales which had once weighed thirty pounds would now weigh fifty. Snow which once reached the first board of the fence would now reach the second. But the alternative was a gradual decline, an acceptance of the decrepitudes of approaching old age – and that was unthinkable.

Thus it was that we called the long-suffering real estate agent who had found us our two previous houses. He is a gentle soul who has made his home in the US after leaving his native Romania. Remarkably he preserves the straightforwardness and logical approach which he needed for his former job, that of engineer. He is literal and honest in his appraisal of properties, whether we are buyers or sellers. Mircea is, in short, a breath of fresh air. But he is most at home in the suburbs. He has a range of Mercedes cars, from which he picks according to the weather and the state of the roads, and he dresses in well-tailored suits, complete with waistcoat and tie. His shoes are gorgeous, probably made in Italy, and the sort of accoutrements one sees in the glossy magazine of the New York Times. They are not the shoes to tramp the muddy countryside of mid-Winter Maryland but that is what we asked him to do.

After triaging a number of properties we found one in a secluded, rural area which turned out to be the epicenter of Northern Maryland fox-hunting. Its appeal lay in having a modest-sized but attractive, light-filled house, a glorious Amish-built horse barn and, at least on paper, a sizable area of land. But, where was the land? Documents and maps left open on the kitchen table told us emphatically that the large arable field close to the house was *not* part of the property. How, then, could it be 65 acres? The answer was that the former large farm had been dissected piece-by-piece over the years, leaving a property shaped like a gerrymandered political district.

The seller's agent told us that it would take at least an hour-and-a-half to walk the boundaries. He didn't seem keen. Nor did Mircea, who looked at his shoes and squirmed. But Rosie and I were adamant and we stalked off through the wet grass. Deep horse footprints made the walking difficult. We asked if the owner, a single woman, was an avid rider but were told that it was not any horse of hers which made these treacherous holes but rather that it was the local custom to ride over anyone's land. This turned out to be an understatement as we were to later find out.

After half-a-mile or so the track descended to some bottom lands and we walked along the banks of a small river. The land was peculiarly unkempt with tangles of giant weeds, frozen to a winter gray, and thickets of wild-rose bushes which snatched at us with their thorns. The two agents muttered something about "easements"- a piece of legalese which shapes country life in these parts, as we were to find out. A small stream joined the river, requiring us to balance on the slippery trunk of a fallen tree to make a crossing. On the far side was arable land which had been in corn and some of which went with the property. Rosie and I conferred. Surely we could turn these gray, stalky lands into green pastures and water our cows from this stream?

We decided that the place merited a second look and that we would ask our friend Gary Tanner, a real farmer, to come with us and give us a countryman's point of view. By the time we got back to the house, an hour and forty-five minutes had elapsed and Mircea was walking a little stiffly, with a resolute and frozen smile. After we parted he sat sideways in the driver's seat of his metallic gray Mercedes and tapped his shoes on the driveway with a barely-concealed look of distain.

However Mircea is nothing if not a professional and he was there outside the house, on time and with a smile, when we made a follow-up visit a week later. Arriving in a pickup truck in a fog of diesel smoke was our friend Gary Tanner. Remarkably he knew the seller's agent from the time of his miss-spent youth and soon the two were reminiscing about 'coon hunting in those very woods.

A repeat of the long, soggy walk yielded some answers but provoked more questions. Those scruffy areas along the river were "reconstructed" wet-lands, engineered at state expense and therefore inviolable. Some of the area was in "easement" and couldn't be touched, for fear of fine or gaol; however the seller's agent thought that only a portion was thus encumbered – but nobody was sure. This seemed to us to be an important question. If we were to buy it, could we use the land or not? Getting an answer to this question was to take time and determination.

In the meantime, Rosie asked an heretical question. "What's the use of these wetlands? Why would the state spend good money 'recreating' them when it could be funding Medicaid and programs for women with dependent children?"

Gary Tanner turned towards us with a mischievous smile. "You're a Democrat, Rosie," he replied. "It's a government program – it must be good. It's all part of being *Green*. Don't you want to *Save the Bay*?"

"But how does it do that?" persisted Rosie. "Does it clean the water in some way?"

"It's what's called *Preserving Wildlife Habitat*," explained Gary patiently.

"What sort of wildlife?" asked Rosie. "The only wildlife I can see is Welly." Our Golden Retriever was dashing back and forth through a particularly wet spot, then rolling on his back in a muddy slough.

"Well, you know," said Gary, with a wink. "Bog turtles, newts, all sorts of insects."

"There's some real big snapping turtles in there," added the seller's agent. "You should see the size of some of them females when they come out of the river to lay their eggs. Break a broomstick with their beak, I'm told."

I was just wondering whether tact was a requirement for being a real estate agent when Rosie put her finger on the heart of the matter.

"So, as I see it, the State pays to maintain these bogs, to be a home for these snapping things and mosquitoes, which bite people and give them West Nile disease – and ticks which give them Lyme, come to think of it. Talk about a waste of government money!"

"You've got it all wrong," Gary pointed out. It's not government money, it's *our* money. There you go, thinking like a Democrat again!"

Rosie was not to be drawn into a political argument which she feared she might not win. But the sheer folly of nurturing these noxious creatures still bothered her.

"I mean, what's the use of these creatures, anyway?" she asked. "These bugs and newts and slimy things – not to mention snakes."

I sensed a professorial opportunity. "That's a very anthropo-centric point of view," I pronounced. "All life-forms have value. It's not just a matter of what they can do for humans. They're all unique, they have irreplaceable DNA, they con-tribute to rich and diverse ecosystems."

"La di da. You sound like a National Geographic Special," said Gary. "Now Richard, tell me what you should do if you see a bog turtle?"

"I don't know," I confessed. "Are you telling me I should no-tify the EPA?"

"Lord, no!" replied Gary. "You should shoot it."

"What on earth do you mean?" I asked.

"Come now, professor, even a Ph.D. can understand that. You go to your gun cupboard, take out a 12-guage, load both chambers and let fly."

"But Gary, why would anyone do that?"

"Well Richard, it's simple. It's an endangered species, isn't it? When the Feds or the State ask if you've seen any bog turtles, you can tell them that there are no *live* ones and that way they won't get all over you for having an *endangered species* on your land."

It is impossible to tell when Gary is being serious. He cleared his throat and gestured me to step away from the rest of the party.

"Richard, if you make them an offer, base it just on the house, the barn and the twenty acres near the house. To a farmer, these bottom lands are worthless. Don't offer an extra cent for them."

To this day I don't know whether Gary was being genuinely discreet or merely theatrical. Suffice it to say that, with the loss of hearing that comes with years of riding on tractors, Gary's whispers can be heard in the next field and I have no doubt that the seller's agent registered the conversation and that it improved our bargaining position accordingly.

We told the seller's agent that we would think it over but that we were put off by the thought of using our hard-earned money for the purposes of protecting mosquitoes and turtles, whether snapping or endangered. We left Mircea using a stick to prize cakes of mud off the hand-tooled leather boots which he had worn as a concession to the country life.

2
Horse Dealers

Our hesitations on the purchase of the house were purely for show and in time our offer was accepted. Following Gary Tanner's advice we paid rather little for the bottom-lands: nobody really knew what they were worth and they still don't. Certainly they were never going to be the breadbasket of the state. Instead it was obvious that the long, narrow strip that formed the center of our dumbbell-shaped property was something of a highway for the local horse-riding gentry. It was a mild winter and the strip soon became a morass of muddy hoof-prints.

We had known that we were moving into the heart of Maryland's hunt country and indeed into a rather special, and highly protected, enclave named My Lady's Manor. Gifted by Lord Baltimore to his lady in 1713 it seemed to have resisted the passage of time and reminded me of the English coun-tryside of my youth. I have always felt that we are stewards rather than owners of the land and certainly it was not our intention to stand in the way of local customs.

But the craters made by the horses made walking difficult. It seemed that we should give in and start to ride ourselves: "If you can't beat 'em, join 'em."

Rosie very wisely thought that we should take some riding lessons and really get to know a pair of horses before jumping in to purchase. A horse is a commitment, I was told. It becomes part of the family and you can't just trade it in like a used car.

So we started riding lessons but we also kept an eye open for suitable beasts which were advertised for sale. Here of course the internet has revolutionized shopping. Searches revealed hundreds of possibilities, mostly photographed on green pastures or being jumped by teenaged girls. To a novice equestrian the market seemed strange. Some horses were offered for tens of thousands of dollars; others were in the hundreds, or free to a good home. It was hard to tell any difference by looking at them. Rosie pointed out that they not only differed in bloodlines, which only went so far I thought, but in what they could do – in other words, in how trained they were. Could one not train them, I wondered? That could be time-consuming, I was told, and depended upon temperament. Here I thought I had the answer. The major equine websites had bar-graphs indicating temperament, ranging from 1 (bomb-proof) to 10 (high-strung: excitable). Every horse that looked good was also rated as a 3! It dawned upon me that this rating was self-reported by the owner and that temperament, it seems, is in the eye of the beholder.

An awful lot of these horses were also 9 or 10-years old which, I was told, was neither too young nor too old. Was there a measure of optimism in the way in which these animals were represented, we wondered?

One beast caught our eye – a tall, striking cross between a thoroughbred and a quarter-horse, he was 9 years-old and a number 3 on the scale of temperament.

It may well have been true. The horse was gentle and well-mannered and Rosie and I were sufficiently reassured that we signed on for a monthly lease and some lessons. The owner was the proprietor of a large stable. He was a man of about my age, ruddy in complexion, dressed in blue jeans and cow-boy boots and every inch the outdoors man. Further he pro-jected authority, whether it was a quick slap across the face of an overly friendly horse or a curt reminder to one of his boarders to clean up manure from the barn. He clearly knew his stuff and I was enough of the novice rider that I appreci-ated his didactic teaching style.

The first test was heaving an immense, ornately worked sad-dle on to the back of this tall horse. Our teacher watched out of the corner of his eye and I could not help but wonder whether any of his acolytes failed this test of strength. I passed but only just. Rosie protested that it was a "Western" saddle and that we wanted to ride "English." This was my first hint of a cultural divide in the riding community. We should start by riding Western and then, if we so chose, could switch to English, we were told. Having fond memories of riding in the English style as a young woman, Rosie persisted.

"We've bought a farm in the middle of hunt country and we'll be laughed out of town if we ride on something like *that*." She pointed to the massive saddle with its prominent, phallic leather horn. "Anyway, my husband's an Englishman!"

This brought a twinkle to our host's eye but his opinion was not to be changed. "People fall off English saddles," he said. "Go to an eventing where they're riding English and there's always a paramedic there. You don't see that at Western events."

So Rosie and I took turns at riding the horse around an indoor, then an outdoor, ring. Though he was tall, I did not find the horse intimidating. He walked sedately but could be persuaded to trot by a gentle nudge in the ribs. Our teacher would lean on the fence, taking everything in, and periodically bellow: "Keep your heels down!" or "Shoulders back! Sit up straight!"

We became accustomed to the horse and broached the subject of buying him.

"I would need four thousand five hundred, non-negotiable," said our western friend. "Any horse that knows its stuff is worth that. He's worth at least that much to me for giving lessons. I like having him around. I'm not a horse dealer."

Suddenly another conversation came into my head. Rosie has a relative by marriage, a charming older man of Middle-Eastern origin. His business requires him to be an adept salesperson and he also owns a racehorse or two. The words which were etched on my memory were his, spoken at a family get-together.

"Richard, I do not bull*sheet*. I am not a bull*sheeter*."

Nevertheless a successful businessman and man-about-town. Can you deal in horses and not be a horse-dealer, I began to wonder?

Before completing the purchase we invited one of Rosie's friends to give us a thumbs-up on the horse. She held open his mouth and pronounced "He's got no teeth!" It was not totally true but his teeth were badly formed and quite ground down. "Maybe that's why he's thin," mused Terry. "He finds it difficult to chew."

We decided to think some more about the purchase. How could we have been so naïve, so ignorant? Even if you don't look a gift horse in the mouth, surely you scrutinize the dentition if you're going to expend more than four thousand dollars?

Our interest finally waned when someone directed us to a website in which the horse had been advertised a couple of months previously, by a former owner, and for half the price. It seemed that our western friend was looking for a quick turn-around and a substantial profit. If not a horse dealer, was he perhaps a "bull-*sheeter*?"

At the same time that we were looking for horses for the two of us, Rosie's fertile mind was looking ahead to the prospect of our grandchildren riding a pony around the paddocks. She was convinced that they needed to be weaned from dolls and electronic games and given more exposure to the hurly-burly of the outdoor world. In this I agreed and so we kept our eyes open for a suitable pony. The advice of our expert friends was quite against this: ponies might look cute, they said, but most of them had "snippy" personalities. Far better, we were told, to get the right 15-hand horses and that they would be suitable for grandchildren and Gramps alike.

Nevertheless an advertisement caught our eye and we drove to a farm to see what promised to be a very cute pony. Strangely we were told that our granddaughter could not ride the little guy, who was indeed adorable, but that she could have a riding lesson on another pony, who was not for sale. The owner, a sprightly, fit-looking woman who was just entering her middle years, explained that the pony which we had come to see was suffering from a "stone-bruise" and needed a little time to recover. We were disappointed but sympathetic.

However a serious-looking girl of maybe ten, who was leading a horse past us, muttered darkly: "He's not got a stone-bruise. He's foundered. Everybody knows that."

Rosie was intrigued and asked the girl if this was the first time.

The girl gave us a serious look through her glasses. "Oh no," she said. "He founders all the time." With a sniff of contempt she turned and girl and horse disappeared into a stall.

We asked Terry if "foundering" was a significant problem and were told that we should avoid this pony at all costs. Was this owner also a "horse-dealer"?

But then our luck seemed to change. Terry found two American Paint horses for sale, a 9 year-old gelding and a 13 year-old mare and they were of the right size – 15-hands – and were said to be well trained. The owner Fern was a delight. With a bubbly and outgoing personality she had a resume of such extent and variety that it quite belied her age. Amongst her other accomplishments she was a very experienced rider and had trained horses for the race-track. She was also an ordained minister of the church who solemnized marriages as well as organizing wedding receptions. This was a woman with whom we felt an immediate bond of trust. Indeed she was forthright about the horses and explained that the mare had a little arthritis on one knee which might in time limit her jumping. Inwardly I was thinking that her jumping likely would still be better than mine.

Fern was more interested in finding out about us. As I was a total novice she did not want us buying "too much horse." Rosie and I both tried the horses out in a paddock and had no problems with them. We agreed that I would join Fern for a trail-ride or two before we made any decision.

In the meantime Rosie's friend Babe was looking for a horse, with the intent of keeping it at our place. I suspect that Rosie had been at work here and that she thought that Babe would feel more fulfilled and happier if she picked up this pursuit of their youth. Babe's search led to Fern's farm where there was a thoroughbred for sale. Although he was freshly off the race-track he was described by Fern as being very gentle. He was also absolutely gorgeous and Babe was clearly entranced. Here was the horse of her dreams.

Fern saddled up the lovely animal and rode him to an

enclosed paddock as we followed on foot. As she rode she explained how you could establish yourself as master (or mistress) of the horse by making it do figures-of-eight around trees and circling in the corners of the paddock. We listened and were impressed by the degree of control which she had. The horse was looking better and better in our eyes. Then Fern nudged him to a trot – and the beast threw a series of gigantic bucks. The next moment Fern was lying on the ground and the horse was running off, trying to find an exit from the paddock. Fortunately no bones were broken and Fern was able to ride the horse back to the barn. I felt extremely sympathetic towards her. If one had wanted to stage a demonstration of a horse that was not for the person re-entering the sport, then this could hardly have been bettered.

But did this make Fern yet another horse-dealer? I was inclined to believe that she indeed didn't know that the thoroughbred, which had not been with her for long, was so temperamental and to give her the benefit of the doubt.

3

A Mare Named Dreamy

There was never any question that Dreamy would be my horse. The two paint horses had come as something of a package, with a discounted price, no less, but it was understood that the gelding, Cody, was the better regarded of the two. The young ladies who came most willingly to look after and exercise him referred to him as "Super Cody" because of all the things which he had done in his life but also because of his mischievous sense of humor. Despite having a rotund belly he had credentials as a jumper and he used to be one of those ponies which led the thoroughbreds around the race track.

Dreamy was four years older, had a little arthritis in her knees (who doesn't?) and came along as a companion. She had a reputation for being more of a "beginner's horse" and had apparently taken many people on trail-rides.

Thus it was that the woman who sold us the horses decreed that Dreamy should be my horse. Rosie, who had lots of riding experience, albeit some years ago, should handle the mischievous and more "forward" Cody. Now the seller, Fern, was an impressive person with a great deal of experience both on and off the race-track and her word was that of authority. Dreamy was just the horse for me; besides, she added, mares tended to do better with male riders.

Dreamy and I did a few hour-long trail-rides together before the sale was consummated. The terrain was wooded and the trails sometimes tortuous. We threaded our way around fallen trees, over rocky slopes and often through small streams. Always Fern was in front on some horse she was training, sometimes a mettlesome thoroughbred, and Dreamy and I followed along more or less obediently. She did indeed seem to be a mellow horse and my opinion of myself as a rider began to grow by leaps and bounds.

Occasionally there was a hint that some spirit lurked beneath this calm exterior. Thus when we came to one of these streams, with steep muddy banks, Fern's thoroughbred became fussy and spun circles in the stream, pawing with a forefoot. After many stern admonitions to "walk on," he finally clambered up the far bank and it was our turn. Dreamy sized up the situation for herself and jumped the stream, leaving me clinging to her mane and quite surprised. Clearly I had not been in charge of this situation, but at least I had stayed on.

The horses were duly trucked to our barn and had stalls side by side. Cody did naughty things, like chew on the newly installed wooden gates, and bared his teeth in what looked like a maniacal laugh. Dreamy settled in well and was a delight to be around. Although horses are surely not intelligent creatures, it was very hard to look at those great dark-brown eyes and not discern a depth of feeling and emotion. As I began to know her better and become totally confident that she would not bite, I would no longer turn away to escape the little kisses that she would plant upon my cheek. I began to refer to her as "my girl."

Then came a big day for the family, with the arrival of children and grandchildren from various parts of the country in honor of my younger son's wedding. We had six grandchildren staying with us, of all ages up to seven, and Rosie was looking forward most warmly to the things which we could do together as a family. A big event was to be a picnic down by the river which formed one boundary of our property. There was to be fishing for the little ones, strictly on a "catch and return" basis of course, as the creek is designated as a trout stream, and there were to be pony rides upon the docile Dreamy. Rosie suggested that I should ride her down to the river, a good half-mile away, and that the little ones should walk with their parents. Once reunited, grandchildren would be perched upon Dreamy's saddle and she would be led along by a capable adult. It didn't sound too difficult.

Rosie saddled-up Dreamy, as I was still struggling to master the rat's nest of leather straps and thongs which are referred to as "English tack." Clearly there had been gaps in my education as an Englishman.

I mounted "my girl" with the aid of an upturned plastic bucket, adjusted my reins and instructed her to "walk on." So indeed she did – until we came opposite the barn in which her companion Cody was still incarcerated. His head hung out of the half-door and their eyes met. Some message passed between them and Dreamy suddenly broke into a run. Then down went her head and up came her hindquarters. In vain I pulled back on the reins, hard, which was the only thing I knew to do. She bucked like some caricature of a Wild West bronco: once, twice, three times – and it was all over. I was thrown off, hit the fence with my shoulder and then lay winded upon the ground. Dreamy stopped and I remember feeling grateful that she didn't tread on me. The grandchildren looked on, all safely on the other side of the fence. Welcome to Gramps' and Rosie's farm!

I knew that I was hurt but not badly. After a few seconds of that lightheadedness which comes with physical trauma, I got up and took off my helmet, which was bent. Rosie led Dreamy back to her stall, once again a meek and gentle horse, now that her objective was achieved.

I had no desire to be a party-pooper and so decided to take the tractor down to the bottom-lands so that the picnic could go on. But first I asked for a beer, which is a sovereign remedy for summer-time injuries. In the winter I have found a tot of rum to be more efficacious, as when I fell on a newly-replaced knee at a brother-in-law's Christmas – but that is another story. Willing hands produced a bottle of Loose Cannon beer, which seemed appropriate somehow. It dulled the pain as I eased the tractor over the rutted ground on the way to the creek but it was clear that I had something wrong at the front of my rib-cage and again at the back.

Two days later, when the progeny had departed after a really nice stay, I turned myself in to the doctor, who confirmed broken ribs. I am not a stranger to this condition: indeed, some years previously when I had a CAT scan for a puzzling pneumonia, my physician friend asked a radiologist to read the films. Not knowing that I was in fact a fellow Johns Hopkins faculty member, he commented that the patient was likely "a derelict" on the grounds of the number of old rib-breaks! I imagine that it comes from lying in the gutter and being kicked by passers-by.

One does nothing for the injury (except drink Loose Cannon) and it resolves in six or seven weeks. In the meantime coughs and sneezes mysteriously disappear and laughter is unwise. Choking is to be avoided at all costs as that particular survival reflex is so deep that it is not to be denied.

Meanwhile I looked at Dreamy with wiser eyes. Friends soon learned of her bucking and my fall and assured us that it is a rite of passage in the route to horsemanship. They pronounced Dreamy to be "herd-bound" and were at a bit of a loss as to how to cure this condition. Lauren, the young lady exercise-rider, shrugged and said it was simply that Dreamy was "mare-ish." And there's not much you can do about that.

4
The Ownership of Land

Early one morning, soon after we bought the horses, Rosie and I awoke to a furious barking from Welly the retriever and the sound of thundering hooves. I peeped through the curtains and there were two horsemen, smartly dressed in black coats, trotting past the barn, over the front lawn and off in the direction of "the lower forty." They looked calm but purposeful. Welly looked infuriated and kept up a barrage of barking, feet planted on the top board of the fence. This was his territory and the invasion was an outrage. Meanwhile the two paint horses galloped around the pasture, throwing up their rear ends and doing sideways kicks. To my relief they seemed to have learned the fence pretty well and would slither to a stop just short of the boards, leaving long skid-marks of denuded grass.

This was only the beginning of the morning's activities. From the distance arose an uneery cacophony which our Irish Wolfhound recognized immediately: it was the sound of other hounds and it spoke directly to his soul. He raised his head and let forth a heart-rending series of howls and moans. Welly intervened with his stentorian bark, as he lacks the ability to howl.

The Hunt was in full cry over the nether portions of our property, known to the previous owner as "the lower forty," being forty acres of stream-side land in a rather wild state. Gradually the sound of the hunting horn and the constant chatter of the hounds grew closer and they were clearly coming along a trail that leads through "our" woods and towards the house. Welly had had enough. Fat as he is, he heaved himself over the four-foot fence and headed off in pursuit. He was just out of sight when there arose a dreadful scream. Panicked, I yelled his name at the top of my lungs, convinced that whatever had happened it was Welly's fault. Had he caught the fox? Was the scream from a lady rider who feared that her horse would spook and throw her, faced with Welly's maniacal appearance? We never found out and in due course the retriever returned, all lathered-up but looking proud of himself. Welly had done his duty.

After the hunt was past I walked over the property and found churned up trails and giant "divets." It gave me pause for thought. To what extent is it really our land?

Much of it has restricted use because it is designated wetland and wildlife habitat: that we knew when we bought it. Then there is the point that we are pretty much in the center of fox-hunting country, with our half-mile of river-front being a vital corridor from one wildness to another. Though an informal commitment, it was really just as binding on us to keep this open as to honor the State's piece of paper on wetlands. Rosie and I were certainly in no mood to violate traditions and the sight of the hunt added color to the landscape – not to mention excitement for Welly. And tolerance brought its own rewards. Just as people could ride over our land, so we could ride over theirs. Mostly the countryside was unfenced and you could ride uninterrupted for miles, with just the occasional stream-crossing to add excitement. Where there were fences, the Hunt had installed jumps, for the more adventurous and four-foot gates which could be opened from the saddle, for the more timid.

Our initial disappointment on seeing the plot of the land and learning that the vast 50-acre field beyond the barn was in fact not ours yielded to a certain appreciation. Who could afford to farm the 50 acres himself? It would mean going to the bank for loans on seed and fertilizer, not to mention the cost of equipment. So doubtless, were it ours, we would lease out the bulk of it to a real farmer, as our neighbor was doing. It was all in agricultural preservation and so it would remain unchanged, seeing a yearly alternation of corn and soybeans, and we could enjoy the rolling vistas without having to pay a penny.

I had spent some time and diesel fuel in mowing access trails on the "lower forty" when I received a call one day from a lady member of the hunt. Was it alright, she wanted to know, if they mowed some of the heavy brush to keep open their favorite trails? This was a no-brainer, as it was easier to let someone with bigger equipment hit the hidden logs and rocks and so I gave my assent.

But it did not end like that. A few days later Rosie and I were walking with the dogs – which really means that the dogs were loose and leading the pack – when we heard the sound of heavy machines down by the river. The dogs were barking and looked set to protect us. At first I assumed that the noise was coming from construction on the other side of the river, where our neighbor seems to keep a large workforce perpetually busy. But, no. In front of us, and clearly on our land, a giant yellow shovel was excavating around a little stream which fed into the river. There were two men, one operating the machine and the other, a man of about my age, leaning on a tree and watching. This seemed to me to be a sign of authority and so I approached him and asked him what was going on.

He explained that the previous winter horses and riders had been up to their elbows in mud crossing this little brook and so he had decided to put in a concrete culvert and cover it with twenty tons or so of rock.

It was obvious that the job was near completion and so I had no intention of arguing. In truth there was some advantage to the working as it would allow me to get our tractor to some further land and I was not in any way antagonistic, merely curious. I asked him if he knew that it was our land. He seemed surprised but said that he thought it belonged to the man across the river and that he had given his permission. This seemed somewhat absurd, as the river forms the boundary between two counties and our neighbor certainly must know that it marks the margins of his land, but I let this pass.

Was it a Hunt Club project, I enquired? Were they paying?

Again the gentleman seemed faintly surprised but replied that he supposed that he was paying.

We parted on pleasant terms and Rosie and I walked home with the dogs, pondering the mysteries of country life.

That evening I stopped in on my friend Gary Tanner. "That would have been Uncle Bob," he pronounced. "He's one of the Masters of Hounds. Now, Uncle Bob is a wealthy man. He's in the construction business. But you probably guessed that. He owns the best part of Southern Pennsylvania, I think."

"Do you know how Gary met Uncle Bob?" his wife Joan chimed in. "You tell Richard," she persisted. "You were there."

"Well, Richard, I was driving along Old York when I came across this man standing besides an old pickup truck. Looked like he had broken down, so I stopped."

"Gary always does that," broke in Joan. "Not many people do, these days."

"He told me he had run out of gas," said Gary, "so I told him to hop in and we drove back to the farm to get a can with a gallon or so in it. He was pretty shabby, you know. Not *dirty* – but just shabby. He was pleasant enough and you know I like to talk. I asked him what he was doing in that neck of the woods. He said 'a little of this and a little of that' and I thought he was looking for employment. I told him there was a man a couple of miles down the road who had a big place and might be looking for help. Told him that it might only be casual laboring though."

Gary shifted amongst his pile of bills. "Turns out that it was Uncle Bob – and he *owns* the big place down the road."

I was learning the local cast of characters.

Our land is home to many creatures and some of them are more appealing than snapping turtles. There are fat, waddling groundhogs of course which infuriate the dogs when they are penned on the other side of the fence. There are raccoons which come and raid the garbage at night, so that one has to put heavy rocks on top of the cans. There are beaver down by the river, as evidenced by their murderously effective carpentry work on some of the bankside trees. And there are large numbers of whitetail deer. Mostly we would see these when walking with the dogs. The story was always much the same. Gelert the hound would sense them first and dash away like a racehorse out of the starting gate. Fifty yards away a group of young does would break from cover in the middle of the corn or soybeans, leaping in graceful bounds and flagging danger with their white tails. The hound would be in earnest and would slowly gain on them as they traversed the open space. But the deer were running for their lives and would manage a final leap into dense brush just before the hound caught up. He would maintain the pursuit but, once the prey was in heavy cover, all was lost and he would return minutes later, face flecked with foam and huge tongue lolling. For the next couple of days Gelert would limp stiffly but then all was forgotten and he was ready for the next pursuit.

We had mixed feelings about the deer. They were beautiful to watch but their network of trails through the corn and bean fields bore testimony to how much damage they did to the crops and they provided a host for the notorious deer-tick, which carries the real threat of Lyme disease in our area. So we were willing to listen when a local contractor stopped by and asked if he might lease the deer hunting on our land. He seemed like an intelligent, responsible person and I agreed to walk the property with him. He explained that he was one of a group of four who had some history of hunting together; that they would only use bow and arrow in the woods within three hundred yards of the house and guns in the "lower forty." Further, that rifles were not allowed in the County and that the weapons would be shotguns with solid slugs. The gun season, it transpired, was only two weeks plus a couple of extra days.

Now it seemed to us that we would hardly be aware of gunfire from more than half-a-mile away and that it was pretty obvious that people had hunted that land in previous seasons. The evidence of this was three or four "tree stands" which stared ominously over wood-fringed clearings, albeit looking neglected and vine-covered. Maybe, if the land was going to be hunted anyway, it should be under our control.

But the clincher was the sum of money offered; thousands of dollars for the brief season. It was to be the first income that our farm produced. Maybe there was something to be said for far-flung, wild acres after all.

5
The Hunt Tea

Purely by reason of where we live, and with no other equine distinction whatsoever, we are honorary members of the local Hunt Club. One of the privileges is an invitation to the Landowners' Dinner and, less formally, to the occasional Hunt Tea. The latest invitation was quite memorable.

Rosie and I were attending the Blessing of the Hounds, which is held on the morning of Thanksgiving Day and marks the beginning of the hunting season. This year we had three generations of family with us, not to mention our own hound, Gelert.

The scene is reminiscent of the England of fifty or one hundred years ago and could have been used as a setting for one of the nostalgic British dramas shown on Public Television under the somewhat overblown title of "Masterpiece Theatre." A church dating back to colonial times sits serenely on a knoll, flanked by a graveyard and mature, spreading evergreens and overlooking a large, sloping pasture field. In front of the church is a fenced oval ring, which allows for the promenade of the horses.

Once an obscure country occasion, the Blessing of the Hounds has become quite popular and by the time we arrived there were hundreds of cars, pickups and SUV's parked on the field. Tailgates were lowered and picnics spread, with drinks ranging from light beers to champagne. Our grandchildren joined the others in rolling over and over down the grassy slopes and the ground was pleasantly dry under a warm, bright sun. Not every day in late-November Maryland is this way.

Dogs enjoyed the camaraderie of fellow canines and Gelert was something of a star. His size of course is compelling and we had worked on his coat, which was less tangled than usual. We were ready to be proud of him but we failed to present the dignified appearance that a beast of his stature deserves. Instead we were something of a spectacle. Gelert would make a determined rush towards whatever dog caught his fancy and I would heave back on the leash, determined to prevent his frightening any of these, mainly smaller, beasts or upsetting their owners. But Gelert is stronger than I and the most I could do was to slow him down, rather as a sea-anchor slows a sailboat in a storm, as my feet slid across the grass. Worse, Gelert would make sudden excursions in different directions, such that I was wrapped in leash like a trussed chicken and we provided considerable amusement.

At last the members of the hunt began entering and circling the ring. The horses were immaculate with coats brushed to a lustrous sheen, sometimes close-cropped in patterns, and manes and tails elegantly coiffed. Mostly the horses were well behaved but a few were clearly mettlesome and one rider had to bail out.

The huntsmen came in all shapes and sizes, including children, and I drew some comfort from the fact that some of the older men were not in impressive physical shape; if they could ride with the hunt, might I not too be able to keep up, given sufficient practice?

The riders were resplendent in red or black coats, tight breeches and shining long boots. They circled the enclosure slowly, with some of the lady riders bringing their mounts to a standstill at the fence so that children could pat the horses' heads.

Then one of the red-coated gentlemen, who we later learnt was President of the Hunt, stopped his thoroughbred opposite Rosie and myself and called out, "Nice to see you again! You are coming to the party, Saturday, I hope?" Rosie's brother and son looked at us quizzically. You could almost hear their inner question, 'Are you really a part of this world?'

Reflected glory washed over me: I was beginning to feel at home in this Currier and Ives setting!

Rosie asked where the party was and was told that it was the yellow house on a neighboring road. This brief address would, it proved, be quite sufficient.

Meanwhile the hounds had entered the ring in a noisy rabble but were quietened by a command and sat back on their haunches like soldiers on parade. Our hound Gelert pushed head and neck through the fence to get a better look: he was fascinated by this disciplined behavior and we could only hope that some of it would rub off on him.

Then the huntsmen lined up facing the church and the priest appeared. The blessing was ancient, pretty and quite brief. I recall an invocation that the 'hunters be safe, the hounds swift and the fox elusive.' Ever a champion of the underdog, I found that rather charming.

Then they were off, with a mob of jostling hounds and an orderly succession of horses trotting away into the distance.

Rosie and I resolved to go to the Hunt Tea to which we had been invited. It was on the Saturday after Thanksgiving and was meant to refresh people who had ridden in the lunchtime hunt that day.

It soon became clear why our host had not given a more detailed address. Flanked by horse pastures and reached by a long tree-lined driveway, lay a large yellow house. On one side of the driveway were parked dozens of cars, on the other horse-trailers and pickup trucks.

We rapped the heavy metal knocker and the door was opened by a genial fellow party-goer. Around us swirled people of all ages, many still wearing riding boots but dressed in identical waistcoats and cravats. Rosie assured me that this was the proper attire for hunt social events. Our host and hostess materialized out of nowhere, greeted us warmly and even took our coats. Our sense of wonder began to grow: how could these people have spent the morning and midday hours chasing foxes over muddy fields and then put on such a spread so soon afterwards and be immaculately dressed and yet relaxed? Rosie asked about the provisioning of the food and we were told that our hosts, who like to cook, had prepared it in advance and that the messier things were being done in the garage, to preserve the kitchen in a pristine state. They had catered for an expected three hundred guests! We were in awe at the capability of this couple.

Our host mentioned that he was interested in getting involved in some program which would improve healthcare for the less-advantaged and Rosie's eyes opened wide. She had developed and run a *pro bono* program to bring heart care to people of Grenada and St. Vincent and was acutely aware of the deprivation of healthcare services of most of the population of these islands. Maybe our host would like to do something for the children, she mused? We promised to pursue the topic at a later date and went off in search of a drink.

This was not a difficult quest. There must have been half-a-dozen different marks of Scotch and Bourbon – whiskey galore, indeed – and a separate room set aside for the wine. Duly fortified with Chardonnay and Cabernet we followed the volume of voices to a room with a table loaded down with delectable victuals. Rosie went straight for the shrimp, which were the size of lobster tails, while I favored smoked salmon and then, more guiltily, thinly sliced beef tenderloin. Plates piled high, we headed for some chairs in a living room where an original oil of a hunt scene hung over the fireplace. Before we could sit however we were approached by a sprightly, slim lady of about my age who wanted to know if we rode.

I've never been a multi-tasker and conversing while balancing a wine glass in one hand and a loaded plate in the other was a challenge but the conversation was worth it. Learning that we were novice riders she was full of encouragement and even hinted that in time we might be able to ride in the "back field" with the hunt club. Then she became stern, fixed me with an unwavering gaze, and asked, "Are you limber?"

This quite took the wind out of my sails. As someone who does twenty-five mile cycle rides on our hilly local roads, I think of myself as quite fit for my age. I thought it unlikely that a female contemporary would be stronger – but *limber*? It was not a word which I had heard for years but I thought it had shades of meaning beyond strength; maybe flexibility, and of that I was not quite so confident. Was she talking about the ability to stay in the saddle – or possibly to survive being thrown off?

More encouragement came from an eighty year-old woman who joined us and who still rode with the hunt. It became plain that my being in my late sixties was not going to hold much water as an excuse with these people.

Rosie and I had barely time to catch our breath and manage a mouthful of food before another woman approached us and proclaimed herself one of our neighbors.

"How extraordinary!" she said, looking at me intently. "Come over here," – she gave a gentle tug on my sleeve and led me towards a window. "How extraordinary! In this light the color of your shirt exactly matches the color of your eyes!" She seemed satisfied with this finding and departed abruptly.

"Clearly of an artistic temperament," remarked Rosie, who did not seem so pleased by the close scrutiny of her husband.

And so the afternoon went on. It's invidious to generalize about people but it would be hard to deny that most of our new acquaintances bore their age well, were courteous and friendly, and refreshingly direct in their conversation. Although probably well-off, if not wealthy, there was a lack of ostentation and talk about money. Maybe it was the fact that people shared a love of hunting and of horses and that this overrode their concerns about insurance or commercial real-estate or whatever provided the economic backdrop of this lifestyle.

As we walked back down the driveway, a little unsteadily, we agreed that the afternoon had been great fun. But we were both perplexed by one thing: where was the tea?

6
Yet Another Horse!

Rosie was convinced that, if an exposure to the equestrian lifestyle was stirring my torpid blood, it would also be the saving of her old friend Dolly. The two of them had grown up together and used to ride as teenaged girls: now it seemed that whenever they got together they would swap stories of a crazy thoroughbred named Princess who would run away with them, giving a thrill which would verge on terror. Now Dolly had a neuromuscular ailment which left her struggling with depression. Rosie felt that a return to riding would help her with her strength and coordination and bring the joy of the outdoor world back into her life. Further the responsibility of looking after an animal would give her a purpose; in Rosie's words, it would "take her out of herself." We would provide a stall for the horse but Dolly would be in charge.

The challenge was to find the right horse. Clearly he should be gentle and well trained, as befitted an older rider, but Dolly also wanted a horse with some stature to him. He had to have a bit more height than the Paints which Rosie and I had chosen.

A call from Dolly brought the news: she had bought a Drafthorse/Thoroughbred cross who was so gentle that his owner would put three year-old grandchildren on his back! She had gone ahead and made the commitment and so Rosie and I awaited his arrival with excitement.

A cheery woman arrived with a trailer drawn by a heavy pickup, waking Welly who gave a couple of watch-dog barks. She opened the rear doors and out clattered an enormous animal. Although nominally only "one hand" taller than our Paints, it was as though he were from a different species. Welly launched into a fusillade of barks and even Gelert gave a few gruff warnings; clearly they knew that this was going to be trouble. Dolly offered to take the horse to his stall but the owner declined and marched him into his box, clutching the lead-shank with determination. He tossed his head and whinnied loudly but that seemed to be an understandable response to such an abrupt change of surroundings. Money changed hands and Art belonged to Dolly – and perhaps to us.

Out of caution, and since he was not our horse, we kept Art in a separate pasture from the two Paint horses. He did not like this. Whenever he lost sight of the others he would whinny desperately and run up and down the fence-line. The ground was soft and his feet the size of dinner plates and soon he had converted one side of the paddock into a muddy morass: it seemed that there would be hidden costs to keeping this boy on the place. We were sympathetic to his distress and discussed putting him into the paddock with the other horses but Dolly and her sister were not in favor of this and so he stayed alone. Then one day the Tanner young men were replacing some fence-boards and left open the gate between the two fields. We came home to find the three horses grazing contentedly, side by side, and from that time we never heard another whinny out of Art.

But issues of sex and power soon began to raise their head. Before the arrival of Art, Cody and Dreamy had been something of a unit: they would stand with their noses touching over the fence, lost in some soft equine moment which could last for hours. When left in the same field they would graze contentedly, side by side. All of this changed when the Tanner lads left open the gate and Art's isolation was ended. Dreamy transferred her affections to the tall, dark, handsome stranger and within days it was Cody who was the outcast. He was shunned and usually seen in some far corner of the field, as far away from the new twosome as possible. Now it was not in Cody's nature to be the underdog and he must have felt the loss of his mare keenly. His revenge was to take bites out of Art's backside when the two were being moved around the stalls and the two geldings would go at it, face to face, when separated by a fence. Most worrying were the occasions when Cody managed to trap either of the other two horses in a side aisle of the barn. He would then use his formidably muscled backside to slam the other horse against the gate. By the time I removed the metal gate it had been bent into a crescent shape but fortunately neither horse had been seriously hurt.

Thus we coexisted, wondering whether Rosie's plan to help

Dolly was working out because Art's owner did not come to see him very often. Then one day Rosie persuaded her to come to the farm and, after a very brief circuit around the paddock, Dolly and Art set out on a trail ride with Dreamy and myself. We rode for maybe forty minutes with either one horse or the other in the lead. I found myself in an odd situation, as if I had taken on some mantle of authority which clearly I did not deserve. It was true that I had ridden along these wooded trails and grassy field-verges many times before but always in the company of one of our two young experts. Now I was making the decisions. Some of these were most likely good ones. For instance we did not venture to cross the stream on the wooden bridge, in fear of Art's losing his composure, and we did not trot the horses on the long green verges, as the young ladies liked to do. Instead we kept to a walk, though Art's stature sometimes forced Dreamy into a short trot, to match his walk.

Then we approached a sharp rise which allowed a glimpse of our barn. Art took off at a gallop and Dolly could not hold him back. I struggled to keep control of Dreamy, who span in circles, and so I was too preoccupied to see Dolly fall. By the time I looked up she was lying on the ground and evidently in pain. The "docile" Art looked like the winged horse Pegasus as he crested the last slope to the barn.

I slid off Dreamy and ran to Dolly who remained on the ground. I asked how she was and she replied that she was sure that she had broken ribs. The good news was that she was coherent and didn't seem to have hurt her neck or spine. Not knowing how I could get her out of this earthy place, a few hundred yards from home, I jogged back with Dreamy in search of help.

Dolly's sister and Rosie did not need to be told what had happened. Art had torn past them, hooves throwing up clods of earth, and had taken himself back to the barn. Against advice from the rest of us, but quite understandably, Dolly's sister jumped in her Jeep and set off down the muddy track to rescue Dolly. "It's four-wheel drive," she assured us as she sped off.

Alas, it was not enough. On a muddy bend the vehicle slid to the side and ended up in the pile of manure which we had been building all season. As people are wont to do in such circumstances, she gunned the engine and the front wheels span and sank deeper and deeper into the pile of excreta. Clearly she was not going any further.

There was nothing for it but to get Dolly back under her own power and this Rosie did, walking her ever so slowly and taking as much of her weight as she could.

As for her sister's vehicle, I pulled it out of the manure with our tractor, using a piece of chain procured by one of "our" deer hunters, who happened to be passing by and whose vehicles are better equipped than ours.

Dolly went to a doc-in-a-box in the suburbs where they confirmed that she did indeed have several broken ribs. She was sufficiently disillusioned with Art that she put him up for sale.

Rosie and I talked the incident over with the young ladies,

both of whom had ridden Art, and some strands of consensus began to emerge. The horse was "barn sour", so much was clear. Should we have been more prepared when we came in sight of the farmstead? Absolutely. Should Dolly have worked more with the horse in the paddock before taking him out in wide-open countryside? Yes, again.

Was the horse hopeless? Here the young ladies disagreed. Lauren thought that he didn't know very much: it was as though he had never got beyond first grade. He was not a "made" horse. Could he be made, if we had the time and skill? Probably not, as he was fourteen years old – and she clearly thought that we didn't have the skill. Emily thought that he was simply "a bonehead" – but a great, big, lovable one.

7
A Houdini of a Dog

Welly knows his place in the scheme of things and it is to sit on the threshold outside the barn and let all passers-by know that it is his territory, all his. Here there is a clash with his owners who believe that he should spend the daylight hours in a stall in the barn with his fellow hound and with access to one, but only one, fenced pasture. How Welly addresses this problem is the subject of this chapter but before I spill the beans it is important to say a little about the dog himself.

"Welly" is short for "Wellington," as in the Duke of Wellington, and we must have had premonitions of his delusions of grandeur when we named him. Welly was a Christmas present from me to Rosie and this has led, for the last four years, to dark murmurings to the effect of "For Heaven's sake, give me a sweater or something" when we approach the festive season. Welly came from the Tanner's farm and, inasmuch as he was the only pup out of nine which was not spoken-for when I approached Joan, he could be said to have been the runt of the litter. Welly does not believe this. Although he has been able throughout his life to run under Gelert the Wolfhound, he clearly thinks of himself as the alpha dog. As he approached sexual maturity he began to growl at Gelert and bare his teeth in the most alarming way. Mainly Gelert remained calm but Welly's canines certainly frightened me. Aggressive ear-licking was his other trick, which again Gelert usually tolerated. Sometimes Gelert would take the offensive and become the licker himself, but this would elicit frightening snarls from Welly. Sometimes Gelert would present the other ear and this had an almost Biblical resonance.

Rosie was worried about Welly's aggression and was certain that we should get him "fixed." I swear that women entertain this idea far too easily; men tend to be squeamish and I was opposed. It was all play, I insisted; it was ritual fighting between males who were struggling for dominance. Gelert was by far the larger dog but Welly *knew* that he was in charge; it was a situation which was bound to give rise to rivalry.

Then one day Gelert snapped. The two dogs and I were in the family room when Welly must have overstepped the limit. Suddenly both dogs were standing upright on their hindlegs snapping at one another. They were so fast that the fight was a blur, like the fights in one of those old Popeye cartoons. I stood up from my chair, yelling at them to stop. Instead this whirling, snarling mass of dog wobbled around the room like a spinning top, smashing a table and a lamp and then finally knocking me back into my armchair. I raised an arm in self-defence and it was promptly bitten, and blood spurted from my hand and wrist.

It was not so much the injury itself, which was not as bad as it looked, but rather the thought that one of our dogs had bitten me that I found profoundly unsettling. I told myself that, whichever dog it was, he really didn't mean it and in fact could have done much more damage if he had been in earnest, but it was still upsetting.

This had changed my mind; Welly should be neutered. He was clearly the more aggressive of the two dogs: besides, Gelert was the more valuable of the animals and might one day sire a lineage of famous hounds. He should be kept intact.

An appointment was made for Welly's surgery but then, the next day, came a request from one of Gary Tanner's daughters for Welly to serve as a stud dog. Our reward would be one of the litter, which brought grimaces from Rosie, or a fee of some hundreds of dollars. Welly had a reprieve, if only a short one.

The Tanners asked that we bring Welly over to their place, to spend the weekend with a Golden Retriever bitch which they had bought from a distance away. On seeing Welly the bitch started flagging with her tail that he was an acceptable suitor, and Welly was nothing loath. Although this was his first time his instincts came to the fore and he knew exactly what to do. After he had mounted her, Joan and I wandered away and I drove home, leaving Welly to his nuptial weekend.

That evening the phone rang and it was Joan Tanner.

"Richard, please come and fetch that dog of yours."

I was surprised. "Didn't we say he should stay for a couple of days, to make sure she's impregnated?" I asked.

"Only if you want a vet bill for hundreds of dollars for surgery on his back," Joan replied. "We had a dog like that once before. Really energetic – kept at it all day and threw his back out. Welly's just like that."

I drove across and picked him up, as asked. So that was it: there were other dogs with as great a sex drive as Welly, but very few. Joan Tanner had been breeding dogs for many years and must have seen all sorts of studs. If she thought Welly energetic, I was prepared to believe her.

Despite Welly's obvious ability, Rosie's heart was flinty. He must still make his appointment with the scalpel, which was set for the next week. She explained to me that it was really in Welly's best interests: if he was neutered he could stay with the family he loved and with Gelert; if not, he would have to go.

And so I took him to the local vet, promising him that I would look after him for the rest of his life and yet still feeling pretty rotten.

He was subdued when I picked him up and, I thought, looked reproachful. How easy it is to project our feelings onto our animals! In fact Welly's beautiful dark brown eyes lacked expression and always did. After a couple of days though, he once again sat with his nose in the air, his bearing as regal as ever. In Welly's eyes, he was still the alpha dog.

In due course I went across to the Tanner's farm to see the pups. They were adorable. Strangely nine of them were males and only one a female.

"Welly's a boy-shooter," explained Joan, "or at least he was."

I was under no illusions that I should accept a pup and the Tanner's daughter instead gave me a stud fee, which was enough to buy several Christmas sweaters.

Gary however was not so kind. "Richard, I've always known that you weren't a farmer. No, let me re-phrase that in the elegant words the English use. I've always known that you were challenged when it comes to an understanding of animal husbandry. But you go and make a fine, profitable stud useless?

I didn't know you were stupid."

The first time that Welly and Gelert were confined to a stall in the barn, Welly escaped. I met him halfway between the barn and the house, dragging a leash which he must have taken from a hook in the barn and with his tail wagging nineteen to the dozen. Clearly Welly was pleased with himself.

I examined the stall: I could imagine two escape routes. The outer door was deliberately left open so that the dogs could access one of the pastures at will, giving them room to romp, to select a distant toilet area and to allow them a bit closer to the road, so that they could menace the ladies and gentlemen of the hunt more effectively (I jest). Was he perhaps escaping the pasture by climbing over the four foot-tall wire fence, topped by a single oak board and euphemistically called "no-climb fence" in the real estate listing of the property? It was difficult to imagine.

The alternative route was between the rather widely spaced boards which had been nailed up to form a somewhat Heath Robinson front to the stall and to which was attached a metal gate. With the thought that perhaps he was going between the boards, or using them as steps in a ladder, I resolved to reconstruct the front of the stall and to do it properly. We had recently had a local handyman make stall divisions for the horses and they were solidly constructed of two inch-thick, tongue-and-groove, Southern Pine. Though it was clearly overkill for confining a Golden Retriever, I resolved to use the left-over boards to make a stall front which would match those of the horses. Pleased with the esthetics of this idea, I set to with electric drill, core-bit and four-inch screws to secure these heavy boards to sturdy uprights. The tongue-and-groove mated together nicely and I was soon admiring a wall five feet high and worthy of a concentration camp. Welly was led inside, given a comforting pat on the head and left in his refurbished domain.

I returned to the house and opened a well-deserved beer. A few minutes later Rosie accused me of taking one of her shoes. She knew that she had left them on the porch, outside the back door, and now one was missing. I was mildly offended by this allegation but not provoked sufficiently to leave my beer and search for the missing shoe. Then, out of the corner of my eye, I saw a golden shape moving in front of the barn. Surely, it couldn't be?

There was Welly, shaking something in his mouth in an overdone impression of a terrier shaking a rat. It was of course Rosie's missing dress shoe. Welly relinquished it easily and seemed ecstatically happy to have managed to provoke us – and to have escaped.

I was back to square one. He must be climbing over the "no climb" fence around his acre of pasture. There was only one solution; it was cruel but it would work. We would string an electric fence around the field, on the pasture side and a little below the top wooden board and so out of reach of the little fingers of the grandchildren. I had installed such electric wires when we had previously had a small beef-cattle farm and they had always been effective.

The first step was to visit Smoke at Eastern States and ask for advice. He saw me coming the moment he opened the door and he growled to the two young ladies at the counter: "You've got a customer. He's a minus three."

The girls were perplexed. "He's the professor who wrote about us in that book," explained Smoke patiently. "He made me say things I never said. And he said I was 'vertically challenged.' So now he's a minus three."

I was beginning to catch on. "I didn't know you classified your customers, Smoke. How low does the scale go?"

Smoke raised his head from his records and fixed me with a piercing gaze. He paused a moment for dramatic effect. "Minus three," he said. "It goes as low as minus three."

The young ladies giggled.

"OK, Smoke, you got me. Now, please help me with a pulse-generator for an electric fence."

But Smoke was not finished with me. "As far as I remember, those cows you've got, they're lawn ornaments. Aren't they plywood cut-outs? Seems to me they won't go very far – electric fence or not."

After I had paid my dues, Smoke became helpful, as always. On learning that the fence was for dogs, he helped me select a less powerful generator and wire braided into a sort of plastic yarn, for ease of installation.

In truth the process is quite simple: you nail insulators onto the posts and then string the wire. The only tricky part is ensuring that the pulse-generator is properly earthed and this is done by banging a couple of six foot-long, copper-clad rods into the ground. I have always done these things myself but I was still hurting from my mare's latest temper tantrum and didn't fancy the chore.

Predictably I asked the young Tanner men to help and they arrived in a thunderous pickup and set to work as cheerfully as ever. It wasn't too long before they began to pack away their tools and assured me that it was done. I asked if the fence was producing a good jolt and they pointed to the generator box, where a green light was pulsing.

Decades of work as an experimental scientist have nurtured my skepticism. "Have you checked the wire itself," I asked?

"No way! You don't get me touching one of those things!" John cringed at the very thought.

I replied that I would do it myself and picked up a piece of straw. This I licked and then held to the conductor wire, with about two inches between my fingers and the wire. There was no pulse. Carefully I slid the dampened piece of straw over the conductor until my fingers were almost touching it, and still there was nothing.

"It's a dud," I announced.

"Is that some sort of English trick – the thing with the straw?" asked John Tanner. "Or was that something you picked up in the jungles of Guatemala, working for the Agency?"

John had fallen hook-line-and-sinker for his father's theory that I was a spy in a former life. I was not to be deflected.

"Here, John, you try it. I tell you, it's a dud. Like a damp squib on the 5th of November."

This tough, robust young man would no sooner touch the wire, even with a piece of straw, than he would give up his guns or pay the IRS more than he owed.

So I slid the straw over the wire, somewhat gingerly I have to confess, until my finger touched the conductor. I felt a faint buzz. This was not going to deter Welly!

After walking the perimeter of the field looking for shorts or bad contacts we decided that the yarn-like conductor must be the problem. If so, it would be the first bad advice I had received from Smoke. The young men were totally onboard with my suggestion that we replace the plastic conductor with old-fashioned stainless steel wire; possibly because there was no longer any point in putting their fingers to the test and possibly because it meant extra paid work.

In due course real wire was strung around the field and the shock was adequate, though not savage. Certainly it must have surprised Gelert as we heard a yell from him that evening. We knew that he would stay away from the fence in future and we were satisfied that the two dogs were now safe and that the gentlefolk of Monkton could ride their horses down the road without fear of being accosted by a self-righteous Golden Retriever. At last we were confident that Welly was secure.

The next day we received a visit from King David. Perhaps I should explain. Our friend Gary Tanner awarded this title to the farmer who tills a dozen acres of our "lower forty." At first I thought it was recognition that David rents and farms some eight thousand acres in our neck of the woods, which is by Maryland standards a pretty impressive area. But Gary is a religious man and in fact he came up with this moniker because David puts a lighted star on top of his grain silo for the Christmas season, and Gary can therefore see a Star in the East.

King David had come to pay us ground rent, which was much appreciated. Though cordial, those 8000 acres make him a busy man and he didn't stay in the house for long. As he opened the rear door, he uttered a cry of surprise (I wish I could put an expletive in his mouth but that would not be true). One of his heavy work-boots was missing. I looked out towards the barn and there was Welly, with a large black boot in his mouth and dragging on the ground. You could sense his satisfaction: Welly was free again!

I wish there were a neat ending to this story but there is not. Welly continues to escape from the barn though perhaps less often and only when there is a tempting opportunity to create mayhem.

We don't know how he does it.

8

The Mare Goes Too Far

Five months had passed since Dreamy had thrown me and broken ribs were a distant memory. I had done many trail rides on her and they began to follow a certain pattern. Always one of the young ladies would accompany me and she would be in front, riding one of the geldings. Dreamy and I would troop along in the rear: she accepted that this was her place in the order of things and I accepted that it was mine. We would mount outside the barn and head down the driveway to the road, much to the annoyance of Welly who would keep up a frenzy of barking, whether out of jealousy or a warning to me of danger, I was not sure.

There is a lordly feeling that comes from being on the back of a horse. The sheer height of the beast gives one a different perspective; farm buildings which were hidden by hedgerows come into sudden view and one looks down on cars. This is both literal and figurative. We always entered the road with care but from then on my fellow rider conveyed a sense of

supremacy: this was Hunt Country and we were mounted after all. And so we clopped along the blacktop and the occasional vehicle slowed to a snail's pace or took to the verge out
of alarm. Once onto the pasture fields which are so prevalent
in our area we would look for long, flattish straights and urge
our mounts to a trot. I began to get the hang of "posting,"
or slightly raising my weight off the saddle, when Dreamy's
left shoulder came forward. Though the speed was not great
compared to my cycling outings, the sensation of speed was
there because of the palpable power of the beast and I had
to confess to an exhilaration, to a raising of the spirits. And of
course there was always the lingering apprehension that the
horse would not slow down when instructed to do so.

In truth, although there was a pattern to these rides, there
were also always differences, even surprises. It's a bit like taking out your sailboat on a familiar body of water: the wind is
always different, the light is different and the antics of other
watercraft never cease to surprise.

So it was with the horses. One day we would be trotting and
thinking of slowing to a walk as we approached a hill and the
gelding in front would instead break into a canter. Dreamy
would instantly follow and for a hundred yards or so I would
concentrate on staying in the saddle. Only when Lauren or
Emily had reined in the gelding would I manage to slow
Dreamy down.

The largest horse, Art, was also the most easily frightened.
He would baulk at crossing muddy streams, paw the ground
and spin in circles. It took the expertise of Emily or Lauren to

persuade him to cross and I knew that I could not have done so. Dreamy was less timid but still managed to worry me on occasion because she would sometimes stumble in these stream crossings and there was a momentary fear of pitching forward over her head.

Art was also easily spooked by creatures a fraction of his size. The sudden appearance of a deer in the hedgerow would be all that it took: Art would do a great start and violently throw his head from side to side. Dreamy would invariably take her cue from the male and she would react explosively, throwing her head around and spinning in rapid circles. Always apprehensive, I nevertheless managed to stay in the saddle during these encounters. The young ladies declared that Richard was really doing extremely well.

For my part, I found that there was a feeling of accomplishment on sliding off the horse outside the barn on our return. There was the sense of having faced challenges and of having surmounted them that comes when one ties up the sailboat in its slip after a breezy day. There it is the vagaries of wind and tide, and lurking crab traps, whereas here the obstacles are streams and groundhog holes but the real challenge lies in the temperament of the beast. And Dreamy could be difficult to predict.

One day in early December Lauren and I took Art and Dreamy for a ride. Both horses were slow but gradually woke up after a trot or two. Then, far in the distance, arose the sound of the

Basset hounds. The horses grew more and more agitated and started tossing their heads and spinning in circles. Lauren, who is an expert rider, had difficulty controlling the large, strong Art and she dismounted. Discretion is the better part of valor and I followed suit. Together we walked the horses in the direction of home while the wild cries of the Bassets sounded in the distance. Our route led across a stream with muddy, horse-torn banks and I was loth to ruin my new leather shoes which I use in place of riding boots. I suggested to Lauren that we should re-mount now that the horses had settled down a bit.

This proved to be a strain for me, as I was now riding with shortened stirrups, and it was with some difficulty that I clambered onto Dreamy from the soggy ground. Lauren, though athletic, is not very tall and Art is an imposing horse. Thus Lauren walked him away towards a jump in a nearby fence, which gave her a couple of feet of advantage. Dreamy was unhappy at losing sight of the gelding and reacted explosively. One giant, unexpected buck and I was thrown off and landed on my back on the ground. I saw stars just for a moment and then the real horror began. Dreamy had done another buck, had lost her footing and was falling towards me. Descending from feet above me was this giant, muscled haunch.

I cannot say that my whole life flashed before me but I do remember thinking that there could be no good outcome. She hit me from knee to pelvis with a massive blow, rose to her feet and ran off.

"Oh my God!" cried Lauren, as she reached for her cell phone to call emergency services.

"I'm hurt but I'm OK," I responded. "You don't need to call 911."

I got to my feet, aching hugely but evidently with no long bones broken. I saw no choice but to walk the horses home and plugged on through the mud. The new leather shoes were no longer an issue as we forded the stream. I became disoriented and insisted that we head in one direction until Lauren pointed out that she could see our barn, in the diametric opposite.

Once home, the customary Loose Cannon beer eased my aches and I declined to go to the emergency room. I don't like to wait at the best of times and waiting in a hospital ER comes close to the worst of times. A fortnight later, with no improvement in the pain, I went to a dedicated radiology center in the suburbs. The report came back that I had a line of luminosity (lucidity?) in one of the pelvic bones, consistent with a fracture which was not displaced. Our family doctor, reached by phone, prescribed a quiet life and predicted twelve weeks of healing. Initially he was opposed to my travelling two days later but, faced with the argument that I was planning to go to tropical warmth in Grenada, sit under a palm tree and drink rum punch, he relented.

"When your wife suggests a walk along the beach, let her go on her own," were his parting words.

That is what we did.

9

They Don't Complain

There was something wrong with Gelert the hound. He had a bit of stiffness in his hindquarters and he was so very lethargic. He lay on the thick rubber stall-mat which gives the dogs a bit of comfort in the barn and he panted. Now this was the height of the Maryland summer and you would expect him to be hot but were not his ears too hot? Then there was his complete lack of energy: If I stroked his head he would in turn lick my hand but ever so slowly.

Rosie thought he had Lyme disease, which is the scourge of our area and affects both man and beast alike. In our family we have all had it, with the progress of the disease sharply different depending on when it is first spotted.

Rosie was right. I took the hound into our local vet – fortunately he was able, just, to climb into the back of the SUV – and she did a blood test on the spot. He was strongly positive, which would explain his fever and also his limp. She gave us a vial of doxycycline pills, after starting the treatment with an intramuscular injection of antibiotic.

Rosie and I expected that he would bounce right back within 48 hours, just as Welly had done when he had a bout of this disease. But poor Gelert seemed to get no better and I took him back to the vet. She admitted to being puzzled but thought that she should get some blood tests done, in case it was something quite different, like kidney disease.

Now it was a Friday and, as she had to send the blood to an outside lab, it would be Monday before she had the results. We spent an anxious weekend comforting the hound, who remained lethargic but oh, so sweet. I swear that you could see his misery in those big, expressive eyes of his.

First thing Monday morning we called the vet. The blood work had indeed come back from the lab and it was horrible. Gelert had a blood creatinine level which was twenty-times the normal upper limit and a blood phosphate level which was generally thought to be incompatible with life. Gelert was in end-stage kidney disease, probably as the result of a kidney infection.

Now the vet had some intuition on the Friday that he might have a kidney infection, as well as Lyme disease, and so she had already switched him to a broad-spectrum penicillin derivative. At this point there was nothing further to be done except to give him intravenous antibiotics but this would mean hospitalizing the hound and this she couldn't do, given her small practice.

She had just given him an injection, I forget of what nature, when she left the room muttering: "Five is not enough." I asked her if she was not confident of the volume of the injection but she replied: "No, it's not that. I was just thinking that five years of life is not enough. That's why I could never have one of these dogs. Their lifespan is just so short and it breaks your heart."

I'm often slow to act and indeed we should have picked up on Gelert's disease and sought attention earlier. But some words wake me up, and these words were uncomfortably close to the language of the Ward Sister in Trinidad when the paralysis of Guillain-Barre Syndrome was stealing Rosie's ability to breathe and the nurses could not raise a doctor. "It's in God's hands," was what they had said – and that had sent me running off down the corridor in an unorthodox search for help.

Now I was not willing to let Gelert die and neither was Rosie. We decided to take him to a much larger vet practice which we had used fifteen years earlier, when last we had lived in the area and had Irish Wolfhounds.

To my amazement one of the vets recognized me, remembered the pain of the premature death of one of those long-gone hounds and switched into over-drive. The treatment became aggressive, with Gelert hospitalized for the next three days and given antibiotics through an intravenous drip. She also did a long-overdue urine analysis, which showed lots of protein, red blood cells and generally the horrors of a serious kidney infection.

The vet was truly outstanding in calling us whenever there

was a change in Gelert's condition or treatment. It was very reassuring that they cared so much. Then came a long holiday weekend when the animal hospital had reduced staffing and we opted to look after Gelert at home. This meant pills, lots of huge pills, but also subcutaneous injections of large amounts of fluid which rehydrated him and restored his electrolytes. One of us would infuse the bag-full of fluid beneath his skin, producing a giant bulge which gradually subsided. Throughout all of this there was not a murmur of discontent from Gelert.

To everyone's surprise he became much better. After a brief second stay with the vet the hound which I came to collect walked with a jaunty step, had a freshly groomed coat and sported a large ribbon!

But before the whole episode was over, I had a talking-to from Dr. Splendissima. Though not the lady vet who had remembered me, she was the owner of the practice and had also been much involved in Gelert's care.

A petite, utterly charming woman with sparkling eyes, she gave me some advice on diet for a dog with kidneys which had taken such a major hit. Then she asked why we had kept him intact and I answered with possibly unrealistic hopes about finding a suitable female hound and raising their progeny.

She gave short shrift to these pious hopes. "You can't guarantee you'll get the same lovely personality in the pups, you know," she said. "Better to go out and buy a 5 month-old, when you know what you are getting.

Besides, older males who've not been neutered are much more likely to get prostatitis. Gelert probably had a urinary tract infection which ascended into his kidneys. Prostatitis may have been a factor."

She fixed me with a very steady gaze. "It's the same with older men. You probably know about an enlarged prostate? You really don't need them, do you?"

What on earth was this woman asking?

"You're saying: 'Off with his balls'?" I asked, a trifle shocked.

"You've got it," replied Dr. Splendissima, with a smile.

10

Beneath the Heel of the Government

Gary Tanner was incensed. "There's no way a farmer can make a living in this state. All these regulations – you're damned if you do and damned if you don't. And all these forms – you need a Ph.D. in bureaucracy to survive. Now, King Richard, you're a smart man, you've got a Ph.D., you tell me what you think of this."

Gary couldn't sit down for this conversation, as there were no chairs in the joint kitchen/living room of his house. Indeed there was no sink, no ceiling and no covering to the walls, which looked like the wattle-and-daub of a medieval English house. What had started as a simple plea from his wife Joan for replacement of kitchen cabinets had blossomed into a major renovation in the capable hands of the couple's sons.

To their great credit, neither Gary nor Joan seemed the least upset by the devastation of their surroundings and Gary, as always, was willing to take time for some conversation and some philosophy. I stood leaning against a rough-hewn beam in the denuded wall and Joan tidied up where her sink once had been.

"King Richard, let me give you some background," Gary began. I should add that my regal label always rather mystified me but I thought it might have derived from my telling Gary that I had been born in Bosworth, in Leicestershire, and that the only thing that had ever happened in the little village was that Richard the Third had lost his crown there, in the Wars of the Roses. To be associated with the hunchback villain of Shakespeare's play was not altogether flattering but Gary was fond of the moniker.

"You know that farm up north of here where the buffalo roam and never is heard a dispiriting word?" he asked.

I admitted that I did and that, when feeling particularly vigorous, I would cycle up the hill to the place and stare at the great beasts.

"Well, a logger approached the owner and suggested harvesting timber from a 5-acre parcel. The farmer agreed, the place yielded some nice lumber and he earned thirty thousand dollars."

"That sounds great. Now I know what I'll do to cushion my retirement," I replied.

"Not so fast, King Richard. Not without a permit. You see, he didn't have a permit. Do you know what the County is fining him?"

I had no idea. "Two-fifty, maybe five hundred dollars?' I hazarded.

"One hundred and eighty thousand dollars. They're fining him one hundred and eighty thousand dollars!"

There was a pause as we took in the magnitude of this calamity. "Can't he appeal that?" I was grasping at straws. "How could he possibly pay that?"

"Sell the farm, I would guess." Gary was somber. "Do you know what the thing is – the *irony*, as I suppose an educated man like you would say? He *did* apply for a permit but he was told he was one day late. One day! And that the County would have approved the logging.

King Richard, I tell you, I'm going to buy a place in Kentucky and get away from all this nonsense."

"But, Gary, you've told me this before. Seems to me I saw surveyor's stakes on your place."

"And I was going to move, Richard, I really was. But do you know what happened?"

I confessed that I did not.

"That Governor of ours – he who follows in the footsteps of the Great Tyrant – do you know what he came up with?"

Again I fell short.

"The *Septic Bill.*" Gary's voice dripped with distain. "That Goody Two Shoes has decided that we can only sell two lots, instead of the seven that we've always been allowed. Because the people in Annapolis don't like the idea of more septic tanks. What do you think that does to the value of our property?"

"Halves it, I would think," I replied, with rather uncertain math. "I would think that the State should give you compensation. I mean, I can understand wanting to slow down housing development in rural areas but you can't just arbitrarily tell people that you are devaluing their land."

"You're damned right," growled Gary. "It's theft."

I was beginning to understand Gary's contempt for government. "But who is the Great Tyrant – the inspiration for our present Governor?"

"Who do you think?" Gary likes to be the one who is asking the questions.

"Oh, I don't know. Hitler, Stalin – maybe Genghis Khan?"

"Wrong again - Abraham Lincoln. He was the Great Tyrant. Proclaimed the freedom of slaves which weren't his to free, and didn't free the slaves owned by his friends. We don't revere his memory here in The South. Did you know I was a Confederate soldier in a movie last year?"

Somehow I was not surprised.

"But Gary, back to your moving further south. I suspect that your roots here are just too deep. And I don't want you to go! Who would help me with my cows? What would happen if I borrow a bloody great bull and my little heifer can't give birth? With you gone, we'd have no James Herriot!"

Gary did not respond to the compliment. "We've made an offer on a hundred acres near the Ohio River," he said. "It costs three thousand an acre and they've had good yields of wheat. We'll have to see what happens."

Sobered, I left the worksite, so deep in thought that I fell over a wheelbarrow filled with cement.

Not long after this conversation I was in the bar of the local tavern which is in truth a rather genteel place, serving good food and generously decorated with pictures and paraphernalia of the hunting scene. A blazing log fire completed the winter décor.

Seated next to me on high stools were a thirty-something man sporting an unruly beard and a serious-looking woman of about the same age with glasses and bangs. On the back of their stools hung, rather precariously, winter coats from LL Bean. The man was talking seriously and the woman was watching him intently.

"It's phosphorus that's the real culprit," the young man remarked. "These farmers dump it on the land like it's going out of style and it runs off into the Bay, where it feeds the algae. Algae give lots of bacteria, somehow, and then you get 'dead zones.' It's called *eutrophication*."

"I'm impressed, Bob," the young woman smiled. "How on earth does anyone remember a word like that?"

"There was an article today by that guy in the Sun paper," he replied. "He laid it all out. Phosphorus is toxic. And it's artificial. It's made by agribusiness. It's just that the farmers don't keep up with things. They should be going organic. Put back into the land just what you take out and the land will look after you."

It was on the tip of my tongue to break into this conversation. It was after all a bar, where a certain informality was expected. I wanted to say that farmers don't waste fertilizer; their bottom line is too precarious for that. I wanted to point out to him that in the early years of the 20th century there were ten-times as many dairy farms in the watershed of the Bay and yet there were also ten-times more oysters and the water quality was much better. It didn't look as though farm run-off was the problem. I wanted to ask him if he lived in a suburban development on a half-acre lot and used a lawn-care company to ensure that his grass was a spotless green. Did they use "chemicals" that washed off into the Bay?

But I was inhibited because I was thirty years his senior and would surely have come across as professorial and possibly as boorish. Besides the young woman was clearly enrapt by his information and I didn't want to get into an "old bull, young bull" situation.

But help was at hand. I had noticed that the weathered-looking man on the far side of the couple had been growing increasingly antsy as Bob's monologue had proceeded. He looked faintly familiar and I thought I might have seen him at Eastern States. As the food arrived, he leant across and pointed to Bob's plate, a generously-sized Angus-burger topped with blue cheese.

"Where do you think the beef comes from," he asked? "It's grain-fed, so someone has to grow the grain and he's going to need fertilizer. That includes phosphorus. You want to go organic? You want chicken shit on your burger?"

I raised my beer to my mouth to conceal my amusement and ordered broiled salmon, doubtless farmed but at least some miles offshore from the coast of Maine.

11

Suspicious Truck

One of the delights of living in the country as we do is that one can leave the doors of the house unlocked. Cars sit on the parking lot quite unsecured and containing a debris of scrunched-up dollar bills and coffee-coated quarters, not to mention presents to grandchildren and electrocardiogram patches. There is a freedom which comes from the complete lack of concern over violence or theft.

So it was a shock to come home from the gym one morning and find the house in disarray. Rosie and I had both been out for an hour or so, going our separate ways, and so there had been no vehicles on the parking lot. At first we each blamed the other, at least inwardly. I assumed that Rosie had left open all of the drawers of the desk and filing cabinet, in some frantic search for an elusive piece of paper. It seemed uncharacteristically cavalier of her. Rosie assumed that I had dumped the contents of her jewelry box on the middle of the bed but claims also to have been surprised by my lack of courtesy.

The truth sank in to us at the same moment: we had been burgled!

It was hard to find out what was missing. Although the drawers containing expensive cameras, GPS units and so on, had been opened, none of these things had been taken. Neither had the brand-new laptop on the kitchen counter or the flat-screen TV. It seemed that someone was maybe looking for documents but checkbooks and passports were in plain view and untouched. Bizarrely a ceramic pot filled with change was missing. The thing must have weighed ten pounds and contained only coins of low value, unspent out of laziness, and some British pounds and euros which must have mystified the thief. Quite unnoticed, and now moved, was a box of ancient coins with silver *denarii* of Imperial Rome and *tetradrachmas* of Syracuse and Athens.

Much the same story greeted Rosie in the bedroom. A pillowcase had gone, presumably to hold the loot, but the only jewelry missing was the least expensive. The thief either had poor taste or had been disturbed!

The only other thing which had been taken was a bottle of oxycodone pills, which I had been given after the last broken bones and had not used. So it seemed that we had a thief of modest ambitions, taking piles of change, costume jewelry and a rather weak prescription painkiller.

The local police were prompt and diligent. After an initial visit from a uniformed officer we were visited twice by detectives. They wanted to know of course whether the house had been locked and were not at all surprised that it had not. It was probably a good thing, they remarked, as these particular thieves normally broke a door or a window if the house was locked.

Unaccustomed to being burgled Rosie and I had closed desk drawers and picked up boxes before realizing what had happened and so obliterated useful fingerprints. The only print left was the impression of a nose on the kitchen window. Clearly someone had peered in from the porch and this leant a human, and somewhat unnerving, aspect to the affair. Having watched too many episodes of Investigation and Discovery on the television, Rosie wanted to know if it was possible to do a DNA analysis of the noseprint. She was gently reminded that this might strain the budget of the local force and that no murder had in fact been committed.

Even as the police were still at the house, neighbors began to stop by. Evidently there had been a rash of home burglaries in the area and people were understandably interested. Suspicion centered on a white pickup truck which had been seen driving too slowly along our country lane. It had been seen to park in the mouth of someone's driveway; it had been seen to reverse over someone's grass. It did, or did not, have some sort of local government or utility insignia on the side. One intrepid neighbor had followed the truck half-way to York, Pennsylvania, admitting coyly to the policeman that he had been forced to break the speed limit to stay in contact. He had noted down part of a tag number. The police jotted all of this down and days later it emerged that the truck was indeed a utility vehicle, that its owner did indeed live in the neighborhood and that he had been trying to help the local residents by improving the ragged verges of our road.

But the clouds of suspicion had only just begun to darken the sky. A local electronic chat-room was just becoming popular and it soon began to light up with accounts of local burglaries. It seemed that we had been lucky. Not only did these thieves stave in backdoors if they found them to be locked, they also tended to cut the electrical supply wires to a house so as to put any home security system out of operation. It sounded as though the damage that they did was often more costly than the thievery itself.

With the number of reports came a blizzard of sightings of suspicious vehicles. The most favored was a red pickup truck which had been seen with two occupants, *sitting close together*. I couldn't see why this was suspicious but I was treated with scorn. It was obvious that there *had* been a third person and that he was at large, carrying out depredations, and that he would re-unite with his buddies in the truck. The clincher in this argument was that the men in the truck were young and *weasely-looking*, with straggly beards. Not that we are prejudicial in this neck of the woods.

The hunt for the guilty pickup was to cramp the style of our friend Gary Tanner. He called up one night to enquire about the progress of our fencing and then added, slyly: "You know that we farm some land up route 439? Do you know there's a police cruiser sitting in most every farm drive-way between here and there?"

I confessed I did not, having less reason to drive up that way.

"Well, Richard, do you know what color my pickups are?"

"Don't tell me that they're red and white!"

"You've got it. Now, do you think I want to be pulled over?"

"Gary, they're not going to be interested in your Nutrient Management or whether your dog kennels are within two hundred feet of the road!"

"Very funny, Richard. What about my tags? They're for farm use. And the last I saw of my driver's license, it was on the kitchen countertop. But the boys busted all of that out."

I had forgotten the remodeling of the Tanner's kitchen. And so Gary had to take a roundabout route to the land which he was renting until the police apprehended a suspect and the neighborhood heaved a sigh of relief.

Gary was not convinced it was the right man because Gary didn't entirely trust the police.

"OK, Gary, I know that some of you former Confederates don't like Government. But, surely, local police are different, aren't they?"

Gary paused a moment while he banged on one of the outlets of his seed-drill which was blocked. The drill was hitched to one of Gary's classic red tractors, which throbbed steadily with only the occasional convulsion, and we were looking over one of our paddocks which horses and a wet Spring had turned into a morass. Gary put down his wrench and looked me square in the eye.

"King Richard, do you remember the red barn which used to adorn Millersville?" Gary added emphasis to the word *adorn*, to make it plain that it was not only the professor who could enjoy the subtleties of the language.

"Of course, Gary," I replied. "It was a landmark – the center of Millersville. Half of Millersville, in fact. I couldn't believe it when it burned down."

"Well, that was our barn and the police thought that *we* had burned it down."

I was taken aback. "I can't believe that. I mean, you're a Christian, a pillar of local society – and I bet you didn't have any insurance on it."

"Well, I did, Richard, but not much. Anyway they had their cross-hairs fixed on me. Asked me if I would come in and take a polygraph test. But first they wanted to interview me and they said it would be recorded. So I went into the station and sat in their little room and in comes a detective and he sits down, takes out a recorder and puts it on the table in front of me. 'For your information, Mr. Tanner, this interview will be recorded,' he says. So I take my recorder out of my pocket, put it down on the table and say, 'For your information, Officer, this interview will be recorded'! Do you know, Richard, he turned quite shirty? I mean, he was really pissed-off. He just stood up and announced that the interview was over. But he asked if I would still come in for the polygraph test. I said I didn't think so. I told him that what's sauce for the goose is sauce for the gander.

I mean, what's happened to the idea of equal rights under the Constitution? Since when does Mr. Joe Citizen lose his rights when he enters a police station?"

12
A Gift Horse

Dreamy had done more damage to me than anyone had suspected. The Grenada visit had come and gone, more weeks had gone by and still I had nagging pains that moved around from hip to lower back to thigh. Eventually I listened to Rosie who had been saying all along that I should go and get myself 'imaged.' An MRI scan was duly performed, insurance was duly billed and my GP was told that I had four fractures of the pelvis. Three of them were on the mend but, given my age, the fourth might never heal!

I will forego any more clinical stuff, as it is a notorious tendency of older folk to talk of bones and joints and of pain medicines. Suffice it to say that I was out of horseback riding for a while but that time does heal.

Dreamy was put up for sale. This raised ethical issues as she had hurt me twice and we really didn't want her hurting anyone else. The first person to show any real interest in her was a single mother with two teenaged daughters who were described as being expert riders. They were looking for a horse for the elder of the girls and it sounded as though it might be a match. I had persuaded myself that my own inexperience was likely part of the problem with Dreamy and that I should, at the very least, have been more sensitive to her moods: an experienced rider might not have re-mounted her after she was upset by the Basset hounds.

When the mother and girls arrived at the barn, I was dismayed. These were not the Amazons I had been expecting but, rather, delicate little girls. The prospective rider was a little shy in getting Dreamy to lift her feet for picking and her mother explained that she had spent some time in the local children's hospital with a punctured lung from an accident with a horse.

I told them that the horse was not the right fit for her. I was damned if I would be a "horse- dealer"!

But we could not afford to keep Dreamy as a big pet and I was not in a position to ride her. A second prospect looked much more promising: she was an experienced rider who was delighted with Dreamy in a couple of trial sessions. I admitted to her that the horse could be temperamental but we both thought that part of the problem was her interaction with the geldings: the purchaser had one other horse, also a mare, and so the dynamics of the herd would be different.

The deal was made and Dreamy walked up into the trailer readily enough. The tailgate clanged shut and she was gone.

I was surprisingly sad about her going. Although she had been offhand with me for a couple of weeks after the bucking episode, she had gradually come round and long before she was sold she had returned to her former affectionate behavior, the soft whinnies and the little kisses. Further she had been "my horse;" my introduction into the world of riding and one had to admit that it had not ended well.

Knowing that the new owner was a prolific user of Facebook, I conquered my aversion to "social media" and joined that site so as to follow Dreamy's fate. I never posted anything myself and my role was strictly that of voyeur. To my delight I found that Dreamy and her new owner were bonding well and that there had been no untoward incidents. It was time for me to move on.

Months passed and friends in the neighborhood said that they were on the lookout for a new horse for me. He should be older and well-trained, maybe a retired hunter. A quarter-horse was thought to be ideal, as less highly-strung than a thoroughbred, and he should be of medium size, somewhere between fifteen and sixteen hands.

Word came from a friend who lives close-by that he had indeed found a suitable horse and that, if he suited, he would be free to us. He was not exactly a "rescue horse" but his owner, a well-known trainer of race-horses, had become seriously ill and wanted someone to look after a favorite mount. By now it was no surprise to us that a horseman, facing very difficult health issues of his own, would think of the welfare of his horse, nor that the local community would feel responsible for placing the horse in comfortable surroundings: this was how people thought of their horses. Placing the horse with Rosie and myself promised to be of benefit to both man and beast and so we acquiesced readily enough.

In a continuing story of kindness, a former lady Master of Hounds of the local hunt collected the horse and brought him over to us in her trailer. She backed up to the barn, Welly sounded his usual alarm, and our benefactor opened the rear door, lead-shank in hand. Out stepped a giant of a white horse, the stuff of mythology. He paused to look around him and then followed his mistress to his stall, every inch a patrician.

This was no quarter-horse; nor was he fifteen- to- sixteen hands. He was a thoroughbred and he was large. Just how large became clear as Dolly led her horse out of the barn, as by coincidence he was to be sold that day and his purchaser had just pulled up. Art was my definition of a tall horse and without question the new arrival was taller.

The lady huntsman returned with a saddle and a bridle of her own and tacked-up the newcomer, whose name was Diamond Jim. She knew that he had not been ridden for eighteen months and was concerned that he might have forgotten his training. As an accomplished rider she wanted to try him out before entrusting him to a novice, or perhaps more telling, entrusting a novice to him. She walked the stately creature out of the barnyard and disappeared down the hill. I held my breath. Fifteen minutes later she re-appeared, dismounted lightly and announced: "He's everything he should be. He's a wise horse but he can be naughty. Knows better than to take advantage of me. Made me feel like a peanut, though."

Thus did Diamond Jim become "our horse," inasmuch as you own any animal. We discovered that he had been a racehorse and that Diamond Jim was his track name. Wanting to forget that period of his life we re-named him "Lord Jim" and he settled in nicely. When our benefactor Liz found out how green I was, she volunteered to help me get accustomed to Lord Jim, which really meant teaching me to ride.

I would jog around the paddock on the huge beast, feeling a little uncertain as he would sometimes throw a tantrum if I didn't meet his standards, perhaps by pulling too hard on his mouth. It was decreed that I should use a "stronger bit" when first I took him out on a trail-ride.

The opportunity came with the arrival of a young woman riding instructor and a pair of her young students. Morgan had brought their horses in her trailer and so together we saddled-up four mounts and headed off into the countryside.

Lord Jim did not like this "stronger bit." He simply came to a halt in the middle of a large field and refused to move. I kicked him, as instructed, but he weighs ten times as much as I and inertia rules. Before I really knew what was happening, Morgan leant over and slapped him in the face. Lord Jim exploded, throwing his head sky-high and circling around. I survived these gyrations but Morgan suggested that I should dismount, which I did, and ride her horse, a beautiful thoroughbred which was just off the track. Thus we all finished the ride, more or less under control.

We had learned that Lord Jim did not like the stronger bit and made a softer adjustment. We had also learned, I thought, that one does not slap him in the face.

As an aristocrat, and Lord Jim is said to have a storied pedigree, Jim expects to be treated properly. We had been warned by Liz that he might not take kindly to being restrained in cross-ties. Despite our warnings, this was exactly what the farrier did when he came to work on Jim's giant hooves. A wild look came into the horse's eye and, with a shake of his head, he broke the halter. Now halters are designed to break under serious stress and the leather thong, which forms the weak link, had indeed let go. The farrier was not to be deterred and selected another halter, made entirely of heavy nylon webbing. Again Lord Jim gave a massive shrug – and this time the rope tied to the barn snapped. This was the sort of line which we use to secure our thirty-foot sailboat!

Jim's eyes were wilder than ever and it was clear that a third attempt at tying him would lead to a torn-down barn or a broken neck. We gave in, and I simply stood at his head holding a limp lead-shank as the farrier put shoes on his front feet. Lord Jim was quiet and obedient. We were treating him with respect and he was responding accordingly.

Gradually Lord Jim and I became accustomed to one another. He would open his mouth to help me in my fumbling attempts to insert the bit, though it still remained a stretch to loop the bridle over his ears. The boy knows some English and you have only to say "trot, trot" and off he goes, with that long stride of his. This horse does not need any encouragement to go. This is all well and good in the paddock but when we are out in the open fields and Lord Jim sees a grass strip stretching in front of him for a couple of furlongs, you can sense his impatience and you know that he remembers his days on the racetrack.

Jim and I are a work in progress and so we do not know how this story will end.

13
Brown Cows Again!

You cannot, I think, keep three dogs and three horses and say that you are a farm, especially if two of the horses are for your own riding and one is a pet. Farmers have a product, usually edible, which benefits mankind and farmers aim to make a profit: judged by these standards, we were falling woefully short. It is not just that one does not want to deceive the Internal Revenue Service; it is a matter of honor to do something useful. Indeed I have friends who farm no more than ten acres and who bristle at being called "hobby farmers." They take this as a demeaning term to use for people who struggle through the mud and snow of winter to fatten steers for the meat auction.

Thus it was that Rosie and I decided that we should have cattle once again. Always ready to romanticize the past, we knew that it should be a cow-calf operation, in which the progeny are your product. And, of course, the cows had to be brown.

We knew where to keep the cattle as we owned some twelve

acres of land at the very end of the property, beyond the river and the wetlands with their mosquitoes and snapping turtles. Access from the house and barn might be a problem, being at best hilly and distant and at worst tortuous and slippery, even dangerous. But Rosie feels that difficulties are there to be overcome and I was complicit in this optimism.

It seemed to us that there were two authorities whom we should consult before enclosing open farmland in the heart of My Lady's Manor; one was the Environmental Protection Agency and their local surrogates, representing The Law, and the other was the Hunt. Both were powerful forces.

We agonized over how to water the cattle; as the field is a good half-mile from the barn, our well was clearly not an option! But there is a stream not far from the area which we planned to enclose and we mused about a solar-powered electric pump to feed a large trough, which would be some-what uphill. Internet searches suggested that this should be possible and gave dimensions of pipe to use, hydrostatic pressure *et cetera*. It would be expensive and we would have to sink the pipe to the trough at least three-and-a-half feet deep, to avoid freezing. Theoretically the trough would not freeze if there was a continuous flow of water but that was theory.

The real reason for this approach of course was to keep the cattle from entering the stream and contaminating it with silt, or worse. I am a lifelong biological scientist and have also enjoyed sailing the Chesapeake Bay for thirty years: fouling the watershed was anathema to me.

When I contacted the Soil Conservation people they were very helpful. A young man came to the farm and walked the whole perimeter with Rosie and myself. As we walked he gave suggestions on how to avoid erosion of the river banks and advice on how extensively we could mow around the wetlands. When we arrived at the planned cattle pasture he fell silent. He was clearly looking at the slope of the land and the vertical drop of the stream. I asked him about solar-powered pumping and he shook his head. Apparently I had touched a sore spot. It seemed that the County used to subsidize such projects but had decided that it was not worth it: too many of the systems failed.

Finances aside, this worried us. This field was quite remote and from time to time Rosie and I go overseas and have someone help look after the place: the last thing which we needed was a failure to provide drinking water which went unnoticed. It seemed wise for us to have a backup plan, with limited access to the stream through a gate which could be opened if there was concern about the pumping or if we left town. The young man agreed and indeed he went further. He thought that the best solution was simply to let the cattle drink from the stream, provided that we had only a half-dozen or so animals on the twelve acres and that we limited the length of the stream which they could reach.

In due course, the Soil Conservation people sent us a letter which reinforced this conclusion. I think that they probably cut us some slack as our project did have a beneficial effect on the watershed as pasture is preferable to sloping croplands, with the soil erosion which occurs during the winter months when the land is bare.

Our dealings with the Hunt were both friendly and humorous. I contacted the Master of Hounds (known as Uncle Bob to the Tanner family) and he immediately offered to help us plan the fencing and position of gates. Clearly he wanted to preserve access for the hunt as much as possible but then we wanted that too. The man is a whirlwind of energy and, admittedly still nursing a healing pelvis, there was no way that I could keep up with him as we stumped across the muddy field. In no time marker stakes were in place and the siting of "jumps" was decided.

Uncle Bob is refreshingly "hands-on" despite his ownership of a large construction company. Let one vignette suffice. As we drove across the field in his pristine SUV, his cell phone rang and there was a brief conversation about his aircraft. Apparently, having put four million into the plane, he was reluctant to spend another half-million on some modification. The call was short and the decision crisply made. Then he went to pounding nails into one of the newly installed "jumps."

The bulk of the fencing was installed by an Amish man, who produced the lower of two bids. A taciturn, though well-humored, man with a long beard, he strode the fields wearing a wide-brimmed black hat and accompanied by his teenaged son. Fascinated by the dictates of the various religions, I quizzed him gently about his operation. Should his son not be in school? No, I was told, he was home-schooled and at fourteen it made more sense for him to be working in the fields. How was it that he could use his bright orange tractor to pound in fence posts so expertly if his religion forbade driving vehicles powered by internal combustion engines? That prohibition, I was told, only applied to the roads. And surely his cell phone stretched the limits of doctrinal tolerance? That was true, I was told, but an exception was made for use in business. Business, it seemed, was worthy and paramount.

One had to admit that they did a great job. The posts were solid and orderly. Wooden boards would have been prohibitively expensive and so we went with five strands of high-tensile wire, with two of the strands electrified.

The power for the fence had to be supplied with a solar panel and I was pleasantly surprised at how good a jolt it gave. But a mile of fence, with some overhanging trees and a stream access, gives lots of scope for shorts. It was many weeks between the building of the fence and the introduction of the cattle and in the meantime the weeds grew exuberantly. Giant pokeweeds towered over the fence and vines descended from overhanging trees and used the fence as a trellis. On a long-delayed inspection visit, there was no fence to be seen in one region; the weeds had encroached from the woods and swallowed it. Clearly something had to be done.

I hacked with shears and experimented with all sorts of weed-whacker heads. It was the height of the humidity of the Maryland summer and sweat poured into my eyes despite the plastic goggles. It was too hot for gloves and so the thorns ripped my hands to shreds. Improbably tall stalks of summer grass wrapped themselves around the head of the weed-whacker and had to be laboriously peeled off, one by one. In memory I was carried back to Grenada and the routine gardeners' chore of cutting back "the bush" with a "cutlass" or machete. A cutlass would have been useful now, I thought.

A week later the weeds were back. A cruder, chemical approach was called for. Rosie and I set off for the fields in the little four wheel-drive truck that the deer hunters left with us, with a fifteen-gallon tank in the bed and a pump driven off the vehicle's battery. I drove as slowly and accurately as possible around the fields while Rosie sat in the bed of the truck and waved her magic wand. In no time at all the fence-line was sprayed and we knew that in a few days we would see the results.

It was a creditable job and in a couple of weeks there was a brown strip maybe six feet wide around the fence. It was ugly but functional.

Heaven forbid that we should poison the stream with herbicide and so we stopped a hundred feet or so from the water: that remaining length would have to be cleared with a weed-whacker – and frequently. We had agonized about how to fence the stream-crossing itself. Our Amish friend had advised that a continuation of the electric wire across the water was the only practicable solution. The shock would be carried by a curtain or frieze of wires that hung from one conductor. Anything more solid would be carried away when the stream flooded and tree branches were carried downstream with the flow.

We were skeptical as to whether such an immaterial barrier would work. Might a cow not just push through it, receive a shock and then simply stay outside the field, in the world at large? Clearly the wires would short out when the stream flooded, as the level came up five feet or so. Would the cows be deterred by the torrent of water itself? It seemed to us that they would really be on probation or in the enclosure "on their own recognizances." If the system was to work at all, we needed to train the cattle under good weather conditions, with the fence doing its job, and then hope that their habits were ingrained by the time of the first flood.

Meanwhile we had to let our newly-seeded pastures establish themselves and so we were not yet in the market for cows – or so we thought. But then the phone rang and it was Gary Tanner.

"Richard, I've found just the animals for you. Now don't say 'no' – just listen. You know you want brown cows and you want something with a little experience?"

"That's what you've found, Gary?" He had my full attention.

"Well, not exactly," Gary admitted. "I've found two beautiful heifers. They're mainly Angus with just a little bit of Jersey in them, just enough to make them docile. They're black but it's really time you got over your prejudice, Richard. Best of all, they're *halter-broke*.

"But Gary, I'm not going to be leading them through town for the 4th of July!"

"Richard, *halter-broke* is important. *When* they escape – not *if* – you can go and fetch them back with some feed. If you go and buy some wild-assed beef cattle and call me to help you round them up, I won't know you."

"So, Gary, if I buy these animals, they come with a warranty, that you'll help me catch them?'

"I'll pick you up tomorrow and we'll go and look at them."

When Gary arrived the next morning he was towing a large cattle trailer and so it seemed as though the decision had already been made. The owner of the heifers was a delightful, vivacious lady who treated us to some wonderful fiddle music in her studio. She played an Appalachian air which had served as a backdrop for the Ken Burns television series on the Civil War and I swear that there was not a dry eye in the place.

Gary agreed on a price per pound for the animals and now I understood: if we did not want them, then he would keep them for himself.

We drove up the road to a local scale and weighed the trailer for a second time. The heifers weighed twenty- two hundred pounds the pair: these were big, plump girls. As we pulled out of the parking area of the grain elevator, the moment of decision arrived. Turn left for the Tanners or right for the Hansfords? Theatrically, Gary jiggled the wheel from side to side.

Rosie and I gave in. The heifers were to be ours. At least, one of them had a little shade of brown on her back.

"As well be hanged for a sheep as a lamb," in the words of my forebears from rural Dorset. We had begun our beef cattle herd with the two heifers, now comfortably at home on a horse pasture near the barn. Why not commit to a couple more animals, when Gary and Joan found them through the local paper?

These cattle were brown! The young cow was a Hereford/Charolais cross and her bull-calf strongly suggested that she had had a tryst with a beef Shorthorn. He was an adorable animal with a luxuriant, mahogany-colored coat. Both mother and son seemed intelligent and alert; I could swear that the cow in particular had a spark in her eye not always seen in cattle.

The animals were bought and named. No longer would we use the Olde English names that decorated our cows a decade-and-a-half ago – no more Buttercup's or Bluebell's. Now the females were named after the fruits of our Grenada years, with the heifers being Mango and PawPaw and the new cow being Kiwi. The little bull was named Cocoa: future male offspring might not be dignified with a name as their days on the farm would be numbered.

Cocoa, at around nine months of age, was still suckling from his mother and the first order of business was to separate the two. This is a noisy business and so we waited until our neighbors were out of town before tricking him to be on the wrong side of a gate. Cocoa and Kiwi were of course outraged and both bellowed for three days. For a while Welly, the Golden Retriever, added to the din but then he gave up.

In time the animals were reunited and happy with their pastures. But the grass didn't last and the new fields which we had seeded and fenced in the Spring were now covered with orchard grass and oats. The time had come to move the animals to their new home. This was a job for the Tanners!

Because our land is so peculiar in shape, or "far-flung" as we like to call it, we would have to load the animals into a trailer, drive a mile down the road and access our fields across a neighbor's property, with his permission. The corn had been combined ("picked") from his fields and the soil was firm; we would do no harm.

Gary backed his trailer up to the barn and I had the animals contained in a side aisle of the building, between gates. Gary and Joan had brought their sons along and so the cattle were faced with a phalanx of waving, gesticulating humans, rather like a Hollywood take of an ancient battle. Three of the animals jumped up into the trailer but Kiwi sensed a trap. From a standing start, she half jumped, half smashed her way through the fence and was loose in the field. The Tanner young men followed and tried to coax her through a gate. But by now Kiwi had perfected her technique and, approaching at a run, cleared the four-foot fence with room to spare! We had, it seemed, a champion jumper.

Sometimes discretion is the better part of valor and Gary

decided that we should be grateful that we had three animals in the trailer and return for Kiwi later.

Fully ten days went by before she began to trust me again and could be tempted into the aisle of the barn with a handful of grain. I called Gary, who turned up with the trailer. Again Kiwi's eyes flashed a message: this was not going to be easy.

Fortunately she made a mistake. She pushed past me and entered a horse stall: I closed the door behind her, shot the bolt and she had nowhere to go but the trailer.

Minutes later she was rejoined with her compatriots, circling the new fields to check out the fencing. Of course we all know that, if she is sufficiently motivated, she can jump it, as it is all four-feet high. As I write this, she has not but has instead assumed the role of matriarch of the little herd, always first to come running across the field when I call them for their grain and always first to push other animals aside at the feed trough. We are happy with her but can't help wondering whether one really wants a cow with that little extra gleam in her eye.

14

A Clash of Cultures

When we bought our farm the appraiser for the bank noted that "there are properties of substantial acreage in the area, which is predominantly rural, but it does not appear that agriculture is the main source of income for the owners." This is undoubtedly true. There are many horse-farms in the area and mainly one sees gorgeous thoroughbreds grazing contentedly on verdant pastures. There are however also large areas of corn, soybeans and "small grains", which change hue with the seasons and these are largely worked on a rental basis by local farmers who till enough land that they can afford large, expensive equipment. There are three local farming families who are dominant in our area and they compete for land to rent, much to the advantage of "landowners" like us. Normally relations between farmers and landowners are cordial and certainly the family who rented our land for the first year were extremely considerate. But occasionally there are glitches and this tale concerns a recent brouhaha, as related to me by Gary Tanner.

We were standing looking over one of our paddocks, elbows on the top board of the fence, and debating how to get our recently acquired cow impregnated. Suddenly Gary changed tack.

"You know those people who live at the end of Taylor Avenue, near the Hunt Club? You must have met them at one of those so-called Hunt Club teas?"

I admitted that I had met them, at exactly such a venue.

"Well, Richard, the gentleman concerned 'took exception', as you Brits would say, to the Snypers running over his lawn on their way to farm the field next door. Now I don't know exactly what they did, maybe just a wheel-mark on the edge of the grass – I don't know. But one day young Snyper was on his combine out in the field and out comes Mr. Taylor driving his fancy new German sedan across the field and stops in front of the combine. He's mad as hell. Not that you believe in Hell, Richard. So Mr. Taylor tells young Snyper that he's going to give him a piece of his mind, that he's fed up about his grass, et cetera.

Young Snyper tells him that he's not interested in a piece of his mind and that he doesn't have the time.

Do you know how we know all this?"

I confessed that I didn't. So far the story promised to be tedious and I shifted my gaze to our newly acquired bull-calf Cocoa who was trying to mount one of the heifers.

"Well, the thing is, young Snyper had turned his fancy

cellphone on and he had a recording, and a video, of the, shall we say 'encounter'?

So here you have Mr. Taylor standing in front of his fancy German car, all bent out of shape, talking up to this young man, way high on the combine.

'Which one of the Snypers are you anyway?' he asks.

'I'm Sam,' the young man replies. 'What is it to you?'

'Well I hear you're as dumb as a pile of rocks,' persists Mr. Taylor.

Well Richard, do you know what happened next? It's all on video and I've seen it but you can't because it's in legal limbo. I guess you can't record someone without their permission in this state.

The car burst into flames!

This took my attention away from the tentative efforts of the bull calf.

"I've got it, Gary! You're going to tell me that this is Divine Intervention!"

"I'd like to, Richard. So, the next thing you hear is Mr. Taylor's wife calling out 'Hon, the car's on fire!'

You see, Richard, the thing is that the Snypers had combined wheat off the field and the straw was laying in windrows. Do you know that word 'windrow'? Might be good for one of your books.

And the straw was all blazing – set fire by the catalytic converter, I guess.

So Mr. Taylor jumps in his car and drives off to the side of his garage. He's probably got a hose there and he thinks he's going to put it out. Can you imagine? The next thing you see, the side of the garage is on fire and then the side of the house! It's vinyl siding and I guess it burns pretty well.

So, do you know what's the last thing you hear on the recording? It's young Snyper calling out, 'Hey, come back! You can't set fire to my field and leave just like that! Come back and put it out!'"

Gary and I all but collapsed at the knees telling one another that it really wasn't funny.

When we recovered I asked him if the car was written-off.

"Sure was, Richard. It was new, too. Top-of-the-line Audi. I hear they're made in Nuremberg. You've probably been there, haven't you, in your work with the Agency?"

I admitted that I had been there, though as a private individual. "It's really a bit grim, Gary. People think of the war crimes trials after the war but it's more the power of the Nazis which you feel. You can imagine the vast rallies they held in that outdoor arena there. I tell you, the ghosts of Hitler and Himmler walk the place."

Gary looked at me. "And you're the one who doesn't believe in Divine Intervention," he said. "What was it – the spontaneous combustion of an Audi?"

15

The Saddest Day

One hot day in early October we had taken the three dogs for a walk and resolved to bathe them. While Welly, the retriever, treats this experience with the langor and pleasure of a hedonist at the spa, Gelert is harder to convince. Only on hot days will he allow himself to be doused and then it has to be with cupsfull from a bucket because he despises the hose. This seemed to be such a day. Despite this, the big hound cried when Rosie gently washed his face and neck. This seemed strange and caught her attention. Always clinically astute, she noticed that he had strange bumps on the side of his nose and she thought that he moved with some discomfort though, Heaven knows, he had been running as fast as the deer a few minutes previously. Did he have some tick-borne infection? We resolved to take him to the vet.

He was seen the next day by a lady vet at the practice whom we had not met before. She examined Gelert, who behaved as always like a perfect gentleman, and then walked him away down the corridor for a second opinion from one of her colleagues.

She returned with a diagnosis which was devastating. It was quite likely that he was suffering from lymphoma, though an infection could not be ruled out. She prescribed a broad-spectrum antibiotic, probably as much for the benefit of the owner as of the hound, and offered to take needle biopsies of two of his lymph nodes. This was done and the hound and I drove off to go home.

Only then did the tears begin to flood down my cheeks. How could this be? The hound was only six years old and he was so fit! This was not a mortally sick-looking animal. Denial appeared on the scene and fought a brief battle with rational thought. Maybe this was an infection from one of those horrible ticks which infested our "bottom lands" and it would eventually give way to one of the weapons in the pharmacist's armory. But I knew that this was not so. The demeanor of the vet had given it away; she had been too kind, too genuinely sad.

Rosie felt the same and we clung to one another for comfort. The hound had been given the steroid prednisone to cut through inflammation and make him more comfortable and we didn't hear another complaint out of him. Instead he returned to his routine of patrolling the perimeter of the paddock and delivering gruff warnings to people riding horses down the road.

The vet called us two days later with the cytology results. The results were what we feared; the hound was suffering from lymphoma.

Both Rosie and I have experience in medical research and we like to think for ourselves. This being the 21st century we flew to the internet and researched canine lymphoma all the way from the authoritative sites like Wikipedia to the personal rants of pet owners who thought they had been let down by their vets. Then we concentrated on lymphoma in Irish Wolfhounds and found very quickly that it is one of the major causes of death. Hovering over all of this was the statistic that male Irish Wolfhounds have an average life expectancy of 6.5 years and Gelert was of course approaching this age. But a more academic website gave a bar-graph which showed which showed that some hounds did indeed live 8 or 9 years and I had always thought that Gelert would have been one of this elite group.

The picture that emerged from the various pet-owners was remarkably consistent – and dire. With no treatment, the hound would live 4 to 6 weeks; with the steroid prednisone alone, he would probably get another month of good life, and with a cocktail of human chemotherapy drugs he might, or might not, get remission for 6 months. In any case, the end would be swift, with massive infiltration of white blood cells into vital organs and failure of the lungs, liver and kidneys.

I talked to Dr. Splendissima, the vet who had saved the dog's life eighteen months ago, and she suggested that we contact an oncology group who were expert in the design of chemotherapeutic regimens. We talked to them and Rosie and

I then faced some big questions. To what extent do you prolong life at any cost, regardless of quality? Is it true that these chemotherapy drugs don't make dogs feel as badly as they make humans feel – or is it just that dogs suffer in silence? Are heroic measures more for the benefit of the owner than for the dog? Can we really afford six-to-eight thousand dollars for chemotherapy?

Lurking in the background behind these discussions were two awkward facts: chemotherapy only worked at all in some dogs and, Gelert was only three months shy of an average lifespan.

We decided to go with just the steroid and, every day thereafter, Gelert received his pill in a ball of cream cheese, which he relished.

With the more certain knowledge that his days were numbered, we savored our time with the hound all the more. His passion of course was to go for walks on our land and that of our neighbors and so we did this more frequently, even when our joints ached and our boots sloshed through glutinous mud. To call these adventures "walks" is perhaps to miss-name them. At a certain distance from the house the hound would be let off the leash and admonished to stay close. This he would do for a while, running ahead and then returning to check up on the slower members of his pack. But inevitably there would come a time when the white tails of leaping deer would flash amongst the corn or beans and the hound would be off in pursuit. The Golden Retriever, Welly, and the new Irish Wolfhound puppy, Tully, would try valiantly to keep up but were outclassed. They would return first and it would be fifteen minutes or so before Gelert came thundering back, often from an unexpected direction, with his face flecked with foam and his huge tongue lolling. The hound was enjoying his life.

Indeed he seemed to be thriving, even becoming stronger. There was a point on our excursions where in the past he had sometimes taken off, with the other dogs in pursuit, and made visits to several other homesteads before returning home from the wrong side of our country lane. This had led to a complaint, albeit a very gentle one, from a neighbor who found the pack of large dogs to be intimidating. Thus for some time I had tried to pre-empt this by putting Gelert back on the leash before reaching the break-away point. This became more and more difficult as his drive for adventure grew. The season was advancing, the ground was freezing hard, and giant tugs from Gelert left me skittering across the ice like a novice water-skier or a Nantucket dory pulled by an angry whale. The hope grew that there was nothing wrong with the hound. More realistically, that the steroid was putting him into a lengthy remission which would allow him to beat the odds.

Gelert is special (I am using the present tense as another is unbearable). All Irish Wolfhounds are gentle and many are intelligent but Gelert has an extra spark of empathy which shows in his eyes. At night we have the dogs with us in the basement and Gelert lies on the floor, with head resting upon elegantly crossed forelegs, watching us. When you speak to him you can see the struggle in his face as he tries desperately to understand, or at least divine your intentions. Certain words resonate powerfully: "bath" elicits a wide-eyed sense of alarm and "Gary" leads to a raising of the ears and a sense of expectation. Gelert spent two weeks of his formative early life with Gary Tanner and his family while we worked on some Caribbean island and has kept a soft spot for Gary, and possibly his wood-burning stove, over the years.

Since it was the winter the dogs spent their nights in the basement where we have a vast crate. For years Gelert and Welly had been crate-mates and had worked out priorities of space and position; between the two of them there was little spare room. They clearly accepted that all rivalries and animosities had to be left aside at the crate door and only when they came out in the morning did they return to their growling, snarling and play wrestling.

With the arrival of Tully, the young female hound, Gelert was banished from the crate. This was because he was the least likely to destroy our possessions in the basement but it seemed (to me) a bit like a betrayal. At first he was confused and tried to push himself into the crate alongside Welly and Tully. But this wouldn't work and after a while he got the hang of sleeping on a rug which we put down, as close as possible to the crate.

The symbolism was bad: the old hound was mortally sick, the young hound was growing by leaps and bounds and she had taken his place in the crate. It looked like Gelert was being replaced. Fortunately I don't believe that hounds have a feeling for symbolism, though I am very sure that they understand jealousy.

Three months had passed since Gelert's diagnosis. Then one morning I found a very sick hound when I went to let the dogs out from the basement. He was breathing rapidly and made little choking movements from time to time; he had no interest in food or water. He got up reluctantly, but loyally, and walked to the barn with the rest of us: the other dogs knew better than to play fight with him. It seemed to Rosie and me that the end was near and we took him to see the vet, Dr. Splendissima. He was able to climb up into the vehicle and his effort was heartbreaking.

The conversation took an unexpected turn. Dr. Splendissima thought it unlikely that this very sudden decline was due to the lymphoma, more likely that it was an additional infection which likely would respond to an antibiotic. She wanted to hospitalize him, so that they could give him intravenous therapy.

I had come with the certain knowledge that this was death by lymphoma and I was distraught. I found it hard to seize hold of this lifeline which was being thrown to us. I was deeply opposed to putting the hound through any extra pain if it was to no good purpose. Rosie was more open-minded and we agreed to let him stay in the practice for the rest of the day: it is hard enough to carry an argument against one strong woman and quite impossible against two.

When I brought the hound home that evening his fever was down a little and he seemed a bit cheerier. That night, as he lay on his side on the basement carpet, I lowered myself onto the floor to spend time with him. Immediately his long tail started to whack the carpet, in pleasure at my attention. Rosie and I went to bed in better spirits and did not cancel the dinner party which we were hosting the next day. The hound was on the mend, if only temporarily.

Next morning I took him back to the vet for further antibiotics, as planned. The expectation was that he would be better that afternoon and that I would come and retrieve him from the vet's just before our dinner party.

Instead there came a call from the vet with very bad news: he was choking more and more, there was a mass in his lungs on X-ray and his little bit of urine was full of blood.

It was time to let him go. I knew this immediately and the vet concurred very fast. This was death from lymphoma and he must have been suffering. Rosie agreed and I drove to the vet's place to see him one last time.

Gelert was lying on the tiled floor, an IV in his foreleg, and breathing with difficulty. As I spoke to him and lay down on the floor beside him, he stretched a little and turned his head towards me with some difficulty. Then he sank back into a more comfortable position and looked away. Death is a private matter.

I lay with him for maybe fifteen minutes, then said goodbye and signed the permission for him to be euthanized. I did not stay to watch him go.

I arrived home ten minutes before the first guests. Somehow Rosie had put on a splendid spread and there was wine in abundance. Oak and maple logs crackled in the fireplace, which cast a welcoming glow. The company was great and fortunately they were dog lovers and they understood. Despite the warm-heartedness and the promise of friendships to blossom in the future though, this was the saddest day.

An Aside – Beddgelert

The technician at the local vet had asked me how Rosie and I had come to name the wolfhound "Gelert." It made an interesting change from Rover and Lassie, she had to admit, but the origin of the name she found curious. In truth it is and thereby hangs a tale.

Some years ago, after Rosie and I had owned wolfhounds but at a time in our lives when we were hound-less, we had taken a trip to Wales. It is a family tradition of ours to go to the UK most years, rent a car and drive the country, staying in bed-and-breakfast places which are always charming and usually historic. On this particular trip we were in the Snowdonia area and, not finding one of our usual mansions, decided to stay in a modest farmhouse in a wild area under a mountain. Asked where we could find a scenic walk, our landlord recommended "the gorge." We followed the track which he indicated and it led to the bank of a mountain river in a narrow defile, shaded by conifers. We eased ourselves over large rocks on the edge of the stream amid the thrilling sounds of a watery cascade. But soon the going became too tough and we were on the point of turning back when I noticed the mouth of an old tunnel that carried an abandoned railway line. Surely we could walk through this and regain the riverside trail when we were past the narrowest part of the ravine?

The tunnel was quite dark and longer than I had hoped. Each footfall was an act of optimism as there was no way of knowing where the ground lay. Rosie in particular had a hard time because she was at the point in her recovery from Guillain-Barre Syndrome at which her foot would sometimes inexplicably droop. Eventually there was a pinprick of light ahead, which was just enough to give us the courage to go on. Sure enough we reached the end of the tunnel and daylight flooded in.

The scene in front of us was spectacular. The sides of the ravine opened out, giving rise to a verdant valley with towering, heather- and gorse-covered mountains as a backdrop. Sure enough, the trail re-emerged along the river and we continued to walk, entranced and quite oblivious to distance covered or thoughts of return. It was one of the most beautiful places I have ever seen and it was quite new to me.

The trail became more cared-for and it looked as though we were approaching a village. A wooden sign-post indicated a detour to "Gelert's Grave" but we ignored this, bent on reaching the village and the inevitable pub. It was time for something to eat. Maybe there would also be a corner shop with a flashlight for the return trip!

The village centered on an old stone bridge crossing the river and consisted of a huddle of houses and a couple of inns, all built out of massive granite blocks. There were also several, rather tasteful, tourist shops and they all seemed to feature images of the head of an Irish Wolfhound! Though the breed is not at all common, we had owned these hounds before and there was no doubt at all in our mind that this was the visage of a wolfhound. There were sculptures in stone and in wood, there were pictures on tea-towels, there was even a wolfhound clock.

Finally the penny dropped. Gelert was a wolfhound! And the village, Beddgelert, was named after this hound!

We resolved that on our walk back we should take the marked detour and visit Gelert's grave.

It was there, standing in the middle of the valley and opposite some large rocks, that we read the story of Gelert.

It seemed that, back in the 13th century, Prince Llewellyn used to hunt with a favorite wolfhound named Gelert. One day he left Gelert back at the camp to guard his infant son. On his return he found the hound standing over the baby and both were dripping with blood. Maddened out of his senses, and thinking that the hound had attacked the infant, he plunged his dagger into Gelert's breast. As the hound lay dying, Llewellyn discovered the body of a wolf behind a nearby rock and realized that Gelert had saved the babe, who was bloodied but unhurt, from the wolf's attack. Appalled that he had killed his loyal hound, Prince Llewellyn was said to never smile again.

As we walked back, with shadows creeping across the floor of the valley, we decided that if we ever were fortunate enough to live with another Irish Wolfhound, we would name him Gelert.

A year later we moved from Grenada back to northern Maryland and found such an animal. We named him Gelert and he was a special, loyal hound.

16

The Riding Instructor

In the aftermath of my bad experience with Dreamy, it seemed to us that there was more to this horseback riding than caught the eye and that maybe I should seek instruction. It soon became clear that I was wandering into an area peopled with strong personalities, who had strong opinions.

The lady Master of Hounds who had helped us acquire our big thoroughbred, Lord Jim, came over to our place a number of times when she realized how green I was and helped me with some of the basics. Doubtless she would have been willing to do more but Rosie and I felt that teaching Riding 101 was maybe a waste of this accomplished equestrian's time.

Liz was firm, with both rider and horse. A typical session would see me mounted on this large animal, walking him around the paddock, while she barked orders.

"Sit up straight! Heels down! Look in the direction you're going! Keep your hands quiet!

Tell him to stop! No – not like that – don't lean forward, sit deep in the saddle! Go easy on his mouth – he doesn't need that much of a command!"

The horse tossed his head, unhappy that I had pulled back too hard on the reins but we came to a stop close enough to Liz.

"You can't stop him by pulling back on the reins," she cautioned. "He weighs ten times as much as you. You just sit back in the saddle, put your weight on your heels and say 'Ho.' He should stop."

"What if he doesn't?"

"You give a gentle pull on the reins, no more than necessary. And release the pressure as soon as he stops. That's his reward for doing the right thing."

After a while I graduated to trotting, initially in circles and tethered to Liz by what I learned was called a "lunge line." To quieten my hands, Liz fitted a strap around the horse's neck and I was told to hold onto this. It was, it seems, part of a "martingale." [Horseback riding, I was learning, has a language all of its own and rivals sailing in the number of terms it has contributed to everyday language. This is fodder for thought and I may chew on it further in a little while].

Things proceeded quietly enough and I was able to practice my "posting", or rising and falling in the saddle with the gait of the horse. Lord Jim and I seemed to be getting along and we were released from the bondage of the lunge line. But then I made the mistake of giving him too strong a command to begin his trot. Jim exploded, as though out of the starting gate in his old days, and my hands went for my security strap and I lost control of the reins. I was in the act of finding them, and probably quite forgetting to put my weight backwards in the saddle, when Liz placed herself in front of the horse and forced him to a stop. She said that Jim was being "naughty": I thought that she was being brave.

Clearly I had much to learn. I also had a new instructor, a young woman who was interested in keeping her horse at our place, and this worked well as Liz was leaving town on some extended trip.

Morgan was also formidable in her own way and brooked nonsense from neither horse nor rider. But her style of riding was quite different! She began with the stirrups which she said were too short and which she lengthened. Liz had said that you should "ride short and love long," or some such salty remark.

And of course you pulled back on the reins to stop the horse! Moreover she didn't trust the bit which Liz had lent us; she didn't think it was "strong enough" to restrain a powerful, "forward" horse. Instead she rigged (nautical expression) a "Kimberwick," which Jim hated. This was as it should be, Morgan thought; a horse is not meant to like the bit.

However Jim had his own way of doing things and would respond with temper tantrums if I pulled back too hard on this strong bit. He would throw his head around with enough power that I soon learned to be very, very gentle.

Morgan is a wonderful instructor, ever watchful and perceptive. But she is more used to teaching pre-teens than seventy year-olds. She issues a continuous flow of suggestions and commands: "Hold his mane when you get up into 2-point! Look where you're going before you get into the turn! Heels down! Hands quiet!" – and so on.

Lessons were meant to be an hour but by thirty minutes I generally had enough. Morgan was sympathetic, saying that all that "posting" and "2-point" would wear out anybody's thighs. I didn't have the heart to tell her that it was not the horse who wore me out, and the thighs which were the weak point; it was she who wore me out and the brain which was fatigued.

To this day I remain faintly concerned about stopping Jim in open country, if he sees an inviting stretch and remembers his race-track or his hunting days. Do I sit back, deep in the saddle, put my weight on my heels and say "Ho"? Or do I pull back on the reins, with gradually increasing pressure?

"Do it all," said Rosie. "And pray."

17

A Cattle Drive

The good thing about Gary Tanner is that he knows his cows and is kind and generous with his advice. The not-so-good thing is that it is next to impossible to know whether he is speaking in earnest or merely pulling the proverbial leg. This dilemma in reading the man came into sharp focus very recently.

We were leaning on the wooden fence inspecting our black heifer, Mango, who had reached her due date, nine months after her encounter with Mr. Surefire, the AI man, and who was beginning to swell with milk. She was laboring across our little fenced "corral" in search of grain, pulling her feet with effort out of fifteen inches or so of mud.

The weather had been bad and was now forecast to become worse. A heavy snow fall had thawed over the last couple of days, leaving wet ice in some places and glutinous mud in others. Now however we were expecting another blast of Canadian air, probably to be dubbed a "polar vortex" by the

TV weathermen, with twenty degrees of frost and twenty-five to forty knots of wind out of the northwest. The chilling effect would be numbing and Mango was ready to give birth.

"King Richard, you've got no choice," began Gary. "You've got nowhere to confine her down here except the corral – and look at it!" He gestured contemptuously towards the sea of mud. "If she gets into trouble, and she is a heifer after all, no vet's going to go in *there* for a difficult birth.

No, you'll just have to walk her to the barn."

I stared at him in disbelief. Was the man serious? We were three-quarters of a mile from our house and barn and the route was hilly and icy in places, low-lying and swampy in others. Even with a well-natured cow, it looked to be an impossibility. Surely Gary was playing with me?

But Gary had a halter with him and began to pantomime lassoing the cow. An uneasiness came over me: could the man be serious?

I turned away to get something from the little truck and when I came back Gary had a bewildered-looking Mango in a halter! He made motions to open the gate and let her out but he didn't look keen. I thought to call his bluff.

"If anyone's going to walk her, Gary, it should be me."

"No, no, King Richard, she won't listen to you. I'll walk her."

With this, Gary led the heifer through the gate and towards the wooden bridge over the stream. She balked on the threshold of the bridge as, in fairness, any thoughtful animal would. Gary was stymied.

I volunteered to walk her through the stream at a ford where local riders cross on horseback. I had boots, Gary had tennis shoes; it seemed only fair. With a show of reluctance Gary handed me the rope halter and insisted that he would take over on the far side of the stream.

Mango hesitated, I gave her a bit of a tug, and in a few steps we were through the water and up a muddy bank. I don't know which of us was more surprised. Now all that we had to do was to keep walking for three-quarters of a mile.

Gary and his wife started up the little truck and followed at a discreet distance, to avoid spooking the heifer. This smooth progress could only last so long and soon enough Mango planted her feet in the mud and refused to move. Now she weighs almost ten-times what I do and so a tug-of-war is quite unequal. I gave her a few seconds, spoke soothingly to her, rubbed the top of her head and then gave the "Coome On" call that I always use when I call the cows for sweet-feed. She stepped forward and we made another hundred yards or so before she again made a stand.

This scenario was repeated over and over again. Meanwhile Gary and Joan lurked in the Kubota truck, just in eye-sight and following the drier ground. Mango and I did not have the luxury of going out of our way to find firmer footing: it was clear that her patience would be sufficiently tried by the shortest route.

We began to climb and Mango's stops began to get more frequent. By turns I soothed and cajoled her. She began to foam at the mouth and her eyes rolled in what I took to be terror. I resorted more and more to simply pulling her, convincing myself that I could not really hurt her with my miniscule strength.

In the middle of a fifty-acre field of corn stubble, covered with a scattering of ice floes and riven by the erosion of a winter's rains, I began to think that I had lost the struggle. She simply would not move. Could it be that all this effort had been in vain? How on earth could we rescue her from here? The ground was too soggy for any truck and trailer and I hated the thought of brutalizing her by pulling her with the tractor.

Finally, with lots of tugging, we made fifty more yards and it was just enough. From the crest of a ridge she saw the board fence around the pasture where she had spent her summer. She recognized it and began to move!

From that point, the struggle was over. We walked through two small paddocks and reached the barn! Some simple bribery with sweet-feed, a quick slamming of a half-door and we had her confined in a stall. Gary re-emerged to help with this final step, his tennis shoes still clean.

"Well, Richard,' he said. "Was that the Boers' revenge?"

I was lagging him in the conversation, as usual.

"Come on, Richard," he admonished. "Didn't you Brits drive the Boers out of their homeland, and they had to set out on The Great Trek? Maybe this was their revenge."

But it was Joan who had the last word.

"Remember when you bought these heifers and you weren't sure you wanted them because they were black?

What did we tell you about how important it was that they were *halter-broke?*"

Mango spent the next four days in a horse stall, becoming more and more irritable. Meanwhile the 40-knot gusts of Arctic air shook the barn and froze the frost-free faucets. Rosie and I went and looked at her every few hours, acutely aware that there was an eight-hour gap overnight when she might well go into labor. We felt guilty but the need for sleep was stronger.

We reached Saturday morning, which promised to be busy as the two "horse ladies" emerged from winter hibernation and planned to come and exercise their mounts. There was also an appointment with a woman who was interested in renting a couple of stalls for her horses.

Mango began to moo and a fluid-filled sack the size of a football emerged from her. Rosie and I have had four children between us and are not strangers to the mysteries of childbirth. We knew of course that things began with "the waters breaking" but were used to a stream of liquid, not the appearance of a great, glistening structure. Could this be normal in cows?

I called Gary and Joan Tanner, who assured me that indeed it was and that they would come across in one hour.

Meanwhile Mango had changed from a Dr. Jeckyll to a Ms. Hyde. She charged the half-door of the stall where I stood watching her and aimed a powerful butt of her head. I moved in time, she smashed into the door, and now her waters really broke. I decided to give her some privacy and wait for the Tanners.

Everyone arrived at once and the barn resembled a busy day at the State Fair. Horses clattered in and out of the aisle and Welly the retriever escaped from his pen and leapt frantically at the half-door of Mango's stall in an attempt to see what was going on.

Two pristine white hooves had emerged from Mango but she had made no more progress for half-an-hour or so, when the Tanners arrived. Gary and Joan declared that she was spooked by all the goings-on and that we should give her some quiet for an hour. We retreated to the house and sat around the kitchen table drinking coffee.

Gary as usual wanted my take on the political issues of the day, which meant the Russian threats to the Crimea.

"King Richard, don't you think an ex-colonel of the KGB out-classes a social worker, community organizer, from Chicago when it comes to getting down-and-dirty? Richard, are you *rootin'* for *Putin*?"

I probably said that I hoped that decency would prevail, or something equally hopeless, and the talk returned to cows.

"Richard, you know when Joan and I came down to your

far-flung field? I like that. Isn't that what you educated people call *alliteration*? And we gave you advice on moving Mango back to the barn? Well, that was in the nature of *veterinary* practice. You remember, Rosie, that you gave us some home-baked cornbread to take home? Well, I was on the phone with daughter Jen last night. She'd just come back from flying some high-priced embryo down to Carolina. I told her not to even think of setting up practice in *The Manor*"

Here Gary gave a leer which conveyed his feelings on our upper-crusty neighborhood.

"I told her they pay their vets in *cornbread*!"

It was time to look again at Mango. She was stuck – and Gary decided we should pull the calf out. While I searched for ropes, Gary again used his cowboy skills to get a halter on her so that we could tie her to a stout post. Without this any attempt to help her would have been suicidal.

With ropes tied tight over the two little hooves, Gary and I pulled, and pulled. The force needed was extraordinary and for a while I thought that it was all in vain. Then a nose emerged and, little by little, the rest of the head. With this, the thing was done. The whole length of the calf emerged and he plopped upon the floor of the stall.

Rosie and I, as nervous first parents, were concerned about whether his airway was clear but there was no need to worry. Mango's instincts took over and made her a great new mother. She licked and licked the little creature while he wriggled and showed every sign of life. Within minutes he was trying to stand on wobbly legs and a little later that afternoon we heard slurping noises as Rosie and I hid behind the stall door. The little fellow was suckling: clearly he was a survivor.

We were thrilled with the new arrival and in awe of Mango's maternal instincts. She was going to be a great mother and we were going to have to be quite careful not to come between her and her little calf.

That evening Joan Tanner called up to ask how cow and calf were doing.

"What are you going to call him?" she asked. "You can't use any of those fancy tropical fruit names you like, since he's a bull calf."

"Well, Joan," I replied. "We think we'll call him *Cornbread*."

18
The Debutantes' Ball

Tully, our female Irish Wolfhound, was coming of age and it was time to find her a suitor. This is not a matter to be taken lightly. We knew enough from our ownership of hounds long gone that one does not simply call a breeder and ask for stud service, any more than one goes to the Internet to purchase a hound in the first place. Money alone is not sufficient: if a breeder has not been introduced to your bitch and approved of her he or she will simply not allow a mating. We were well aware of this. What surprised us in this Spring of 2014 was that the only breeder whom we could locate within 200 miles would not even *sell* us a male puppy without first approving of our bitch. Possibly we had been too forthright in admitting that we wanted for her to have one litter, so that we could give progeny to friends who have much admired the hound; perhaps we should have been more clandestine.

The Wolfhound community justifies this exclusivity on the grounds of "improving the breed," which is something of a

Holy Grail. The cynical might think that they are simply trying to keep themselves in business and the prices up, much like the silversmith's guild of the Middle Ages. But we won't countenance such a view. While true that breeders are thin upon the ground in these Mid-Atlantic states, with North Carolina and Indiana being second-closest after Pennsylvania, it is not true that their puppies are particularly pricey, being much in line with those of other pure-bred dogs.

The long and the short of it was that Tully would have to be "shown." She was thirteen months old and so pretty much a teenager but shows were held on an annual basis and so this made sense for her "coming out." There was a "specialty show" held remarkably close to us (possibly Maryland is regarded as some sort of halfway point, as there is not a single breeder in the state) and hounds would be coming from as far away as Maine and Florida. This was the occasion on which Tully was to be presented to the Wolfhound world.

Like any debutante, she needed to be dressed appropriately, which meant a visit to the groomers at the local vet – a.k.a. "the spa." She came back perfectly coiffed and indeed a different color. Her wheaten coat was altogether lighter than we had realized and she had a reddish tint along her spine which was most becoming. For two long days we tried to keep her out of the mud, as the weather was on the cusp between a particularly snowy winter and a very moist spring. We agreed that the hound was the most beautiful of all those which we had been lucky enough to own; in particular she had a lovely face, with a circle of dark fur setting off her alluring eyes.

The weather for the show however did not look good. The forecast became more and more certain that we were in for heavy rain and a nor'easter of twenty to thirty knots. Rosie and I checked the telephone obsessively, looking for messages of postponement. None came. Joan Tanner who has attended many dog shows, though not for Irish Wolfhounds, assured us that the judging would be moved indoors. I was not so sure: we had taken in two previous shows, with a decade in between, and the format had been identical; the organizers believed in the rules and seemed to be creatures of habit.

The morning of the opening arrived and it was every bit as bad as forecast. We decided to go anyway, with the unworthy thought that, were we the only dog to show in our age-category, then we would win!

The format was indeed the traditional one, with dog-handlers slogging around a grass arena which had been churned to mud. The only shelter from the cold, driving rain was a large tent which housed the officials and which was beginning to flog ominously in the gathering gale.

We checked-in and found that it would be an hour or so before Tully's age-group was shown. It was time to practice; possibly past-time – but no-one has ever accused us of being professionals in our hound ownership. I slipped our newly-purchased show-leash over Tully's head and congratulated myself on its slim elegance. Tully was not so impressed and immediately began to chew on the thin braided nylon. I took it from her mouth and we headed out into the rain to practice our running side-by-side. Now Tully is a bit like Lord Jim the

Thoroughbred in that she likes to go – and go she did. My shoes tore the surface off the wet grass and I fell flat on my face, dragged by a huge hound. We practiced some more and she settled down a little but I was covered in mud from head to toe.

As we waited for our class the tent collapsed. First one of the guy-lines snapped and one corner of the canvas began to flog, then one of the plastic poles broke and the whole thing came down. Fortunately there was time for both hounds and owners to make their escape.

Now these are dedicated people and the show went on. The two lady organizers relocated to a little structure which was probably a score-keeper's hut for ball-games. Still dog-handlers squelched round their circuit and the lady judge brushed at the soaking wet hair which plastered her face.

I felt that at least we had learned from watching the other participants; Tully should be ready for her big moment. But then she was gone – heading straight for the score-keeper's hut. I was left holding a length of the leash, which had indeed broken.

This is where it is useful to be a palpably hopeless male in a sport which is dominated by women. Tully, quite sensibly, had taken refuge in the little hut and the organizers soon found a spare leash which they could lend me. It was of the proper type, unlike our recent internet purchase, and made of leather which should be strong enough to hold the hound. We were back in business.

When our time arrived, the group of us, ten in all, jogged around the soggy perimeter with the handlers sporting slickers and gum boots. No-one fell! Then the hounds were presented individually to the judge, which involved gentle nudging of their limbs until their posture was just right. Stance is everything. When Tully's turn came she walked nicely to the judge, looked her in the eye and then sat down! Wolfhounds seldom sit, even when asked, and this was very much against the rules.

"A moment of comic relief, how nice. I appreciate that," murmured the judge, as I struggled to right the hound. She stood up in time to run her course and acquitted herself quite well.

When the time came for decisions to be made, the judge pointed at hounds other than Tully. We took our bedraggled bodies back to the car and immediately set the heater on full-blast.

We knew that the competition had been stiff and were scarcely surprised that we had not placed in the top three. The first two places were taken by huge animals: Tully was just a smidgeon smaller and the standard for the breed calls for "great stature." Here again, size matters.

There was a second showing on the next day and the scene was quite different. The sun was out and the wind, though stiff, was from a different direction. Handlers were dressed according to unspoken protocols, with the men wearing sports-coats and ties. People had a chance to exchange pleasantries and it became clear to me that it was a small world. If not shown by their breeders, the dogs were shown by professional handlers. I felt quite amateur.

Tully behaved herself well but, facing the same competitors as on the previous day, again failed to place. Nevertheless the day was worthwhile. Tully was praised for her beauty and for her running and I was introduced to a man who turned out to be perhaps the leading breeder on the East Coast. When told that Tully had not placed, he growled "I don't care about that. That's just one judge's opinion. It's my opinion that matters to me." There is perhaps a whiff of arrogance in the Wolfhound community.

I introduced the hound to him and he looked at her critically. "She's a little small but she's got nice ears and a great butt. I'm into butts myself."

This seemed encouraging. Perhaps he would allow a mating with one of his giant gray males or sell us a male pup from a famous lineage. Had Tully's coming-out been a success, after all?

19
Absentee Landlords

Rosie and I have always loved to travel and thought that in our retirement years we would be able to spread our wings more widely. We have also loved animals and their care and upkeep. Now that we have a farm and some large animals we find that these passions do not sit well with one another. It is possible that we should have known this and that to want it all is to be greedy but I don't aim to persevere with this line of thought.

Leaving the farm is difficult. This became plain last month when we took ten days to go to Grenada and celebrate my 70th birthday with old friends and under the tropical sun. We were much relieved to find that Lauren, who was very familiar with the dogs and the horses, would be willing to drop by each day and provide them with food and water. We were leaving on April 23d and so temperatures should be equable enough for the dogs to live comfortably in their stall and the nightmare of frozen pipes in the barn had receded at long last.

However the Spring was late, the ground was cold and the paddocks around the barn were growing so feebly that they could not keep up with the grazing of two horses and a pony. We had also just fed our last bale of hay and there was none available in the vicinity; we were all in the same shape.

But down beyond the stream, three-quarters of a mile away, the 12 acres of cattle pasture was growing well and was more than a match for four head of cattle. The solution seemed clear: the paint/pony cross and the little pony should stay near the barn, where the restricted diet would be good for them as they were both overweight, while Lord Jim, who was looking gaunt and who could be trusted not to over-eat, should go and join the cows in their lush pastures.

Rosie suggested that I should walk him down on a lead-shank but I had memories of walking Mango in the opposite direction and knew how far it could seem. I could also imagine Jim stopping to browse on every green shoot along the way and so I decided to ride him instead.

This doesn't sound like much of a challenge, though it was also true that I had only ever ridden him previously in the company of another horse.

I was quite proud of myself that I was able to tack him up properly and he took the bit easily enough. We set off from the barnyard in good shape and walked down towards the river, resisting the temptation to trot in case he decided to really take off. He crossed the wooden bridge without hesitation and I halted him just short of the cows' enclosure. Slipping off the great beast, I undid the girth and lifted off the saddle. I was relieved that it had gone so well and allowed myself a moment of quiet satisfaction.

Then, before I could open the gate, Jim totally lost it. He took a giant leap in the air, pulled the reins out of my hand and ran off!

Previously, as when he broke his cross-ties, he had not gone far and gave himself up easily enough. This time was different. By the time he reached the bridge he was moving so fast that I heard his hooves clatter and skid over the heavy timbers. He had clearly memorized the route and was heading back for the barn!

I was terrified that he would step on the reins, or catch them round a tree stump, and tear the bit out of his mouth. I jogged back over the rutted fields, in a pale imitation of my cross-country days in the muddy farmland of a wintry Warwickshire. When I arrived Jim was in his paddock, looking quite innocent. My neighbor had apprehended him and brought him back to the barn. Jim was quite unhurt and I can only hope that he didn't put too many deep hoof-prints in my neighbor's perfect lawn.

Lord Jim had voted with his feet: he didn't want to be banished and he may not have liked the cows. But still he needed to go, if he were not to starve while we were away.

By good fortune Lauren arrived that evening to ride her paint pony and I asked her if she would accompany Jim and myself back to the cow fields. She assented readily and again I rode

Jim down to the far-flung area. I expected him to become balky before we even got close but he didn't. Evidently he was happy enough that he was not to be alone. And so Lauren and I rode the two horses through the gate and amongst the curious cows. Lauren rode her horse back through the gate, which I guarded carefully to prevent escape of Jim or cow.

Thus was Jim tricked into living with the cows. I felt no guilt as I believed I was doing the right thing for him and indeed when we brought him back to the barn area two weeks later he looked sleek, almost plump, with nary a rib in sight.

Leaving the cows for a couple of weeks didn't seem reckless or callous: they had grass, a stream and a gourmet salt-block. Until now they had always respected our fence, with its two "hot" wires. But no fence is perfect: the stream might rise and short out the "frieze" of hot wires which guarded the crossing; a limb might fall from a tree and collapse the fence entirely. So, to be cautious, we asked our son Patrick to drive down every other day to make sure that at least the cows were still in the field.

Then there was the pregnancy of Kiwi, the Hereford/Charolais cross. We didn't have an accurate due-date, as she was impregnated by the bull, but I had noticed that her teats were becoming a little more prominent. I mentioned this to Gary Tanner and again the man's good heart got the better of him and he turned up one evening with his wife to take a look at the cow. This was the day before we were due to go to Grenada.

"King Richard, you've got at least two weeks," pronounced Gary, after watching Kiwi jog away across the field.

Relieved, I drove us all back in the little Kubota truck and Rosie and I returned to stuffing things into our suitcases.

The next day was taken up by the journey and we didn't consult our e-mail, in a rare holiday from the 21st century. When we did go online the next day there was a message from Patrick entitled "New Calf." Could he be right, or was he thinking of the little roan bull-calf born a few weeks previously?

There was a photo, e-mailed from his smart phone. Rosie and I squinted at it from all directions, trying to judge the color and the shape of the head. It did indeed look like a new calf and later messages confirmed that it was! Kiwi had a calf and both mother and baby were doing well. So much for Gary Tanner's "two weeks": it had barely been two days! I resolved to rib him without mercy on return from Grenada. But Gary managed to redeem himself.

As soon as we got back I made a quick trip down to the cow pastures and confirmed with my own eyes that we had a new, brown calf. He showed every sign of being a male. That evening I called Gary and he asked me if I knew whether it was a bull calf or a heifer.

"It's a little bull-calf," I replied.

"Are you sure, Richard?"

There was an ominous feeling that I was falling into a trap. "I'm pretty sure," I replied, a little cautiously as I know that in the first few days you can confuse the remains of the umbilical cord with a penis.

"I think you'll find he's a steer," Gary persisted. "We went down there and neutered him for you!"

Later Patrick confirmed that he had bumped into Gary and Joan down at the field, just in time to see Gary drop a lasso neatly over the head of the little bull-calf as he bounded away. It was, by all accounts, worthy of the Wild West.

So Gary gets top marks for his cowboy skills and his kindness but fails in assessing gestational maturity.

Two weeks, indeed!

20
Full Circle

The farm is a work in progress and so there is no obvious place to end these tales. We are ruled by the seasons and although there are subtle differences from year to year, the years are mostly more alike than not. By late-March we will count the remaining hay bales in the loft with growing concern; soon we will have to go raking up the loose stuff. Next year we must buy more. By mid-May we will think that our grass has never looked so luxuriant and the growth will all-but defeat our best efforts at mowing and weed-whacking; but by August it will be brown and sere, the cornflowers will out-grow the grass and we will scan the western sky anxiously for signs of thunder clouds. By late-October we will revel in the colors of the trees, with the maples a brilliant red against the deep yellow of the hickories; but a couple of weeks later we will swear that we have never seen so many leaves in our lives, as they cover the flower-beds in drifts and clog the drains.

There is constancy in the beasts too. Though Gelert the wolf-hound will always be missed, Tully, the young female hound, is beginning to fill his place. Her mischievous sense of humor guarantees her a spot in our hearts.

Lord Jim continues to be kind to me though he is perplexed that I'm not as capable as his former owner and occasionally will show a flash of irritation at my slowness.

Rosie is optimistic that her latest horse will be the right fit. He is a beautiful, older quarter-horse whose owner was keen to give him away as his arthritis was preventing the galloping and jumping which she expects of her mounts. Rosie is looking for a quiet horse who will be reliable on trail-rides and we are hoping that it will be he.

As with the seasons of the farm, I feel that my life has come full-circle, too.

The other day I was mucking out Lord Jim's stall for the umpteenth time. It is hard to credit how much manure one fifteen-hundred pound herbivore can generate in the course of twenty-four hours. Fork after fork of soiled straw was flipped into the wheelbarrow until it was heaped precariously high for the eighty paces or so to the manure heap. This may not sound far but it was a winter's day and the soft tire of the barrow dragged laboriously through the snow. It was hard to imagine on such a day why we had chosen a location so distant from the barn but there was a reason and a good one. Flies pester and infuriate both man and horse during the summer months and so there were rewards in having the manure pile some distance downwind.

In all there were three stalls to be cleaned, as well as a side aisle of the barn. The job allows time for thought and my mind flashed back to my boyhood in the English city of Leicester. We lived in a large Victorian terrace house near to the center of the city. I was five years-old and the country was still hung-over from the Second World War. It was a time of austerity and the British motor industry was yet to re-tool from making tanks and make motor cars widely accessible. In consequence the traffic which passed our front door was quite light and a mixture of frumpy, black pre-war cars, Bedford lorries and horse-drawn carts.

The milkman had a horse who was so familiar with his route that he knew exactly where to stop for each delivery of bottles. The coalman had a heavy cart drawn by two enormous Shire's and they waited patiently as he hefted the hundred-weight sacks of glistening, odiferous coal onto his shoulders and dropped them down into the cellars. Less regularly the rag-and-bone man came through with his insistent cries and his horse too was a huge Shire.

All of these beasts deposited manure in the road and I was given the job, by my father, of nipping out into the road with a bucket and shovel and retrieving the manure. This worried the lady who lived across the street, who used to call out, "Mind the motors! They come so fast!" My father used the manure as fertilizer for his rose bushes and I was remunerated for my work at the rate of one-farthing-a-bucket. Now a farthing was worth a quarter of a penny and there were two hundred and forty pence to the pound. The farthing was a cute little copper coin with a bird on one side with up-cocked tail. Maybe it was a robin, maybe a wren; I'm not sure. On the other side of the coin of course was the head of the King.

Even in those days the farthing was not worth very much and so I had to go to the local baker's shop to exchange my farthings for real money, namely pennies. When I had amassed six pence, I could walk into the city center with my brother and buy a cast-metal farm animal from Woolworths. They had trays of these little things on a counter which was high enough to merit standing on tippy-toe to be able to touch them. The agony of these decisions is with me still. Do you buy a cow or a horse, which was more expensive by tuppence? It never occurred to me that Life was unfair, in that you could not afford them both.

Sixty-five years later I have returned to shoveling horse manure. It goes into a pile which gets pushed into the woods and discarded. Maybe this spring I will use it for my roses.

I have still not decided whether I can afford both horses and cows.